Apolo-WHAT?

Christian Apologetics for the Garden-Variety Pewsitter

By Adam Neubauer

Illustrations by Eli Navarro and Artem Olyfir

Published by Neubauer Enterprises

Apolo-WHAT?: Christian Apologetics for the Garden-Variety Pewsitter

© 2015 by Adam Neubauer

Published by Neubauer Enterprises

All Scripture References: Engelbrecht, Edward. *The Lutheran Study Bible: English Standard Version*. Saint Louis: Concordia Pub. House, 2009.

Acknowledgments

God The Father, and God The Son, and God The Holy Spirit

My entire family and support network

Edited by: Tom Siebert

Proofed, Formatted, and Configured for Publication by: Blake Atwood

Illustrated by:
Eli Navarro: Title Page and Chapters 1-3, 6, 11, 17
Artem Olyfir: Chapters 3.5-5, 7-10, 12-16

CONTENTS

If you are an atheist, agnostic, skeptic, or non-Christian, I recommend that you start with Chapter 2. You are certainly welcome to read the first chapter, which is tailored for practicing Christians. But if you are not a Christian, you may find the first chapter superfluous.

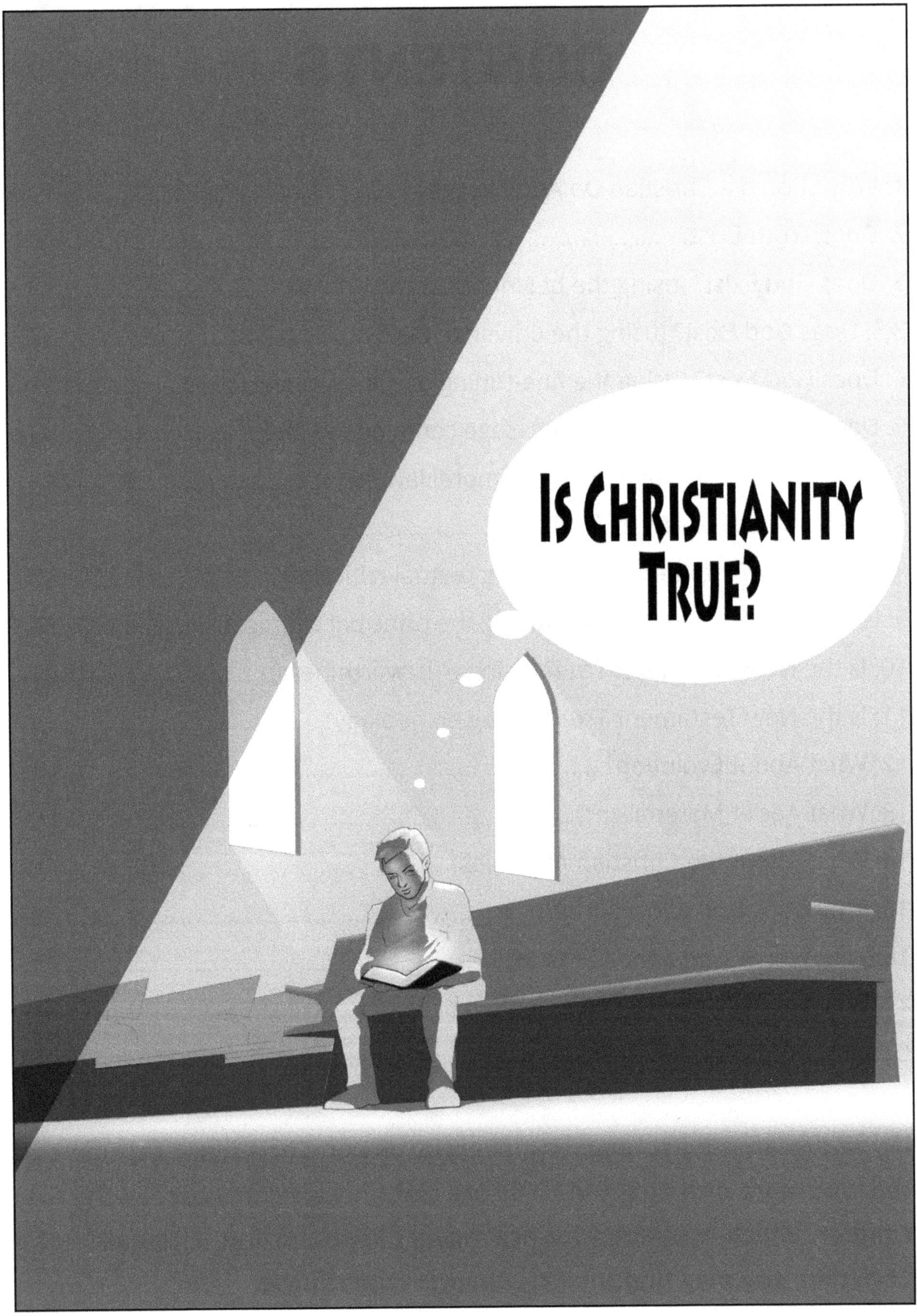
Is Christianity True?

CHAPTER 1

WHY SHOULD A CHRISTIAN DO APOLOGETICS?

Christian apologetics is not apologizing for being a Christian. Christian apologetics is the endeavor of defending Christianity by making a rational presentation of it. Apologetics is derived from the Greek word *apologia*, which means "verbal defense." Apologetics is demonstrating why Christianity is true and defending objections against it.

Let's be clear: You cannot "argue" someone into faith. God alone can endow faith.

Then why should you do apologetics?

Because during the course of contending for Christianity (apologetics), perhaps God can provide faith to the person with whom you are speaking—the listener. (Romans 10:17 – "Faith comes through hearing.")[1]

In most cases your defense does not start by using Scripture. However, if you are advancing your case, then the gospel will eventually emerge as the central point of your message. The problem is that most unbelievers do not accept the Holy Bible as the inerrant Word of God; therefore, you must first build a case exclusive of the Bible and then progressively demonstrate that the Bible is true.

Ultimately, apologetics is providing positive reasons to believe that Christianity is true.

You might be reading this now and saying to yourself: "I don't need reasons; I just have faith." I submit to you that generic faith is not necessarily a virtue. The common atheist has faith that there is no God. Is his faith a virtue? Virtuous faith must be grounded in sound reasoning as well as given by God, both of which are true of the Christian faith. To be an effective apologist, you must understand the intellectual reasons for your faith. I will cover these reasons in greater detail in subsequent chapters.

As for this chapter, I will answer the question: Why should I do apologetics?

If you are a Christian, you are commanded to do apologetics.

Here is specific Scripture supporting the apologetics calling (bold added for emphasis):

1 Peter 3:15 – "In your hearts honor Christ the Lord as holy, **always being prepared to make a defense to anyone who asks you for a reason for the hope that is in you**; yet do it with gentleness and respect."

2 Corinthians 10:5 – "**We destroy arguments and every lofty opinion raised against the knowledge of God**, and take every thought captive to obey Christ."

Jude 1:3 – "Beloved, although I was very eager to write to you about our common salvation, I found it necessary to write appealing to you to **contend for the faith** that was once for all delivered to the saints."

Philippians 1:7 – "It is right for me to feel this way about you all, because I hold you in my heart, for you are all partakers with me of grace, both in my imprisonment and in the **defense and confirmation of the gospel**."

Titus 1:9 – "He must hold firm to the trustworthy word as taught, so that he may be able to give instruction in sound doctrine and also to **rebuke those who contradict it**."

Matthew 10:32-33 – "So everyone who **acknowledges me before men**, I also will acknowledge before my Father who is in heaven, but whoever denies me before men, I also will deny before my Father who is in heaven."

Perhaps the most direct command for apologetics is the greatest commandment:

Mark 12:30 – "(Jesus said,) and you shall love the Lord your God with all your heart and with all your soul and with all your **mind** and with all your strength."

In the greatest commandment (also found in Matthew and Luke), Jesus commands us to love Him with the totality of our **mind**. Surely, our minds are designed by God to use reason and rationale. If we dive into our faith with our mind, our faith will be further enriched by God's precious Word and His magnificent creation.

Another important reason to do Christian apologetics is because we live in an increasingly intrusive and infectious atheistic society. We see it everywhere. Atheists contend for their "faith" (they posit that we live in a godless universe). They convince people to doubt Christianity.

Given the current state of your faith, if an atheist were to ask, "**Why do you believe in God?**" what would you tell him? Think about it for a second. What would you tell him? Is your only response "the Bible"? The atheist doesn't believe in the veracity of the Bible, so your contention will not stand with him.

You need to start from common ground and provide reasons why Christianity is true (yes, one of those reasons is the truth of the Bible, but that is a topic for future chapters).

The following situation arises every single day: A Christian, even your own child, might enter a pluralistic environment (high school, college, job) and an atheist presents compelling reasons **against** Christianity. What are your preventive measures that your child is not snatched away from the faith? Certainly, prayer is one of those measures. Christian apologetics is another weapon. If you and your child are equipped with intellectual reasons for your faith, you will not be easily swayed.

What is a <u>pewsitter</u>? One day several years ago, I was hanging around the narthex after worship service. I overheard (okay, I might have been eavesdropping—yes, I am a sinner!) a discussion between a few active members of the church. They referred to another individual as a "pewsitter." I interrupted their conversation and asked, "What is a pewsitter?" A pewsitter is someone who attends worship services, sits in the pew, gives an offering, and doesn't contribute much more to the church. Maybe the pewsitter attends Bible study or serves as an usher. I still have not made up my mind if "pewsitter" was intended to be a pejorative term in the original discussion. Notwithstanding, I have come to embrace the term "pewsitter."

Most of us (the church at large) are pewsitters. We are laymen. We are commoners. We do not make our living studying Christianity or atheism. We are men and women of other trades.

We are not **expert** Christian apologists, but we still have critical roles in the outcome of the struggle for Christ.

My college education is in the field of history. I studied the American Revolutionary War, which was a fascinating episode in the history of the world. Here is an interesting aspect of the conflict:

The British were experts in warfare. They were one of the strongest world powers at the time of the Revolutionary War. The most common British soldier was an adult (aged 17–25). He also enlisted for lifelong service to the empire, and most of the early British participants in the war had five to fifteen years of previous experience in battle. Even the war-time enlistees received up to two years of training before being deployed to the American theater.[2]

Conversely, the most common American regular in the Continental Army enlisted from ages 14–16 and was drawn from the dredges of society. George Washington received permission from Congress to form this standing army in June of 1775, which means training had to occur in short order. Furthermore, the American militia was a patchwork of tailors, mechanics, farmers, smiths, gentry, common laborers, shopkeepers, clerks, lawyers, and carpenters.[3] All of these men were commoners. They did not make their living in warfare. They were men of other trades. Yet they had an important role in the outcome of the Revolutionary War. The Americans won.

Likewise, we men and women of other trades—we commoners—have an important role in the outcome of the struggle for Christ. The success of the pewsitters will be crucial to the outcome of this pivotal point in Christian history. Just as the merchant, banker, mechanic, factory worker, salesman, tradesman, and farmer won the Revolutionary War, we too must win this war over Christianity.

And of course, all credit goes to God.

I must warn you that the next two chapters may seem a little "dense." If you haven't studied philosophy in a while (or ever), then you might be challenged by the next two chapters. I encourage you to master them. They serve as the fundamentals of Christian apologetics. Just as with any discipline, the fundamentals are critically important.

When you begin to learn mathematics, you don't start with axiomatic set theory and combinatorial geometry. First, you learn simple numbers. You learn the fundamentals. Although these fundamentals may seem difficult at the time, you must learn them prior to moving forward; otherwise, you will have more trouble down the road. It's harder to go back and correct the fundamentals rather than simply learning them correctly in the first place.

The same is true with Christian apologetics. The next two chapters are the fundamentals of Christian apologetics, and it's crucial you learn them.

One of the main purposes of this book is to "whet your palate" to Christian apologetics. For instance, caviar are fish eggs. At one time it was a delicacy reserved for the aristocracy and upper class. Presently, caviar is a more common dish than it was in the past. However, caviar still remains an "acquired taste." The appreciation for caviar is unlikely to be enjoyed by a person (myself included) who has not had substantial exposure to it. Therefore, in order to whet your palate to caviar, you are encouraged to familiarize yourself with a related but less intense version of the food such as salmon. In the same manner, this book is intended to build your exposure and appreciation of Christian apologetics so that you can intensify your study of the material.

In its entirety, the most effective step-by-step process for proving that Christianity is true is contained in the book *I Don't Have Enough Faith to Be an Atheist* by Frank Turek and Norman Geisler.[4] Dr. Turek and Dr. Geisler present a linear stream for the positive case for Christianity. I highly recommend reading that book, after you read this one, of course. I borrowed several components of their outline because it provides the most coherent structure for demonstrating that Christianity is true. We all owe Turek and Geisler a debt of gratitude for designing a bulletproof model for Christian apologetics, a prototype that even I can understand.

Now that we have established the need and the command for Christian apologetics, we can proceed to the first step in presenting a positive case that Christianity is true.

Does truth exist?

This might seem like a simple question with a simple answer, but not everything is what it seems. The next chapter will demonstrate that, yes, truth *does* exist.

CHAPTER 2

DOES TRUTH EXIST?

"What is truth?" - Pontius Pilate (John 18:38)

Pontius Pilate didn't stick around for an answer. He just walked away when Jesus Christ, the living God, told him that all who side with truth hear Jesus' voice. But Pilate doesn't want to listen. Two thousand years later and we still have the same problem. People don't want to hear the truth. Jesus discusses truth many times throughout His ministry (John 1:14, John 1:17, John 8:31–32, John 14:6, John 17:8, John 17:17, Matthew 22:16). God also warns us that people will suppress the truth in unrighteousness to go their own way (Romans 1:18). It's true; in today's culture many deny that any truth exists, let alone the truth of Christianity.

If you are not a Christian, start here:

What is truth?

Truth is that which corresponds to fact or reality. Truth describes an actual state of being, events, or transactions. Despite what you may have heard, truth is absolute. Something that is true is true for all people at all times and in all places.

If you were born on a deserted island without any interaction with anyone for your entire life, you probably would **not** know that the earth is round. But it is still true that the earth is round. Truth is unchanging whether you know the truth or not. Take the deserted island example: no one is on the island to teach you that 2+2=4. Does that mean 2+2=5? Of course not! The truth is that 2+2=4 despite an individual's knowledge of it.

Furthermore, truth does not have to be seen or collected by our senses to be true.

A blind person cannot see the color red. But it is still true that the color red is the color on a stop sign. Red is 620–740 nanometers on the electromagnetic spectrum regardless of whether or not you can see it.

Furthermore, truth is not a human invention.

Gravitational force exists—it is true. Did Isaac Newton invent gravity? No, he merely discovered a truth (gravity) that existed prior to and regardless of human knowledge. Based on these examples, it seems fairly obvious that truth is absolute.

But how do we know truth?

We know truth by the **first principles of thought**. These are self-evident laws of logic. They are immutable. These are laws in the same manner that the laws of physics are laws. These laws do not need to be proven by other laws. They simply exist in reality. You know them so inherently that you probably have never even explicitly examined them unless you have taken philosophy courses.

The first of these laws is the **Law of Identity**. This law holds that a thing is itself and is different from something else. A word or a thing can have only one meaning in one sense in a particular context. This law is so fundamentally apparent that it's almost impossible to explain without simply repeating the definition. This law is the foundation of critical thinking and discussion. This law is the instrument behind apprehension and knowing the definitions of terms. This law enables you to agree upon meanings so that you can communicate.

A square is a square and not a circle. A married man is married and not a bachelor. A squared circle does not exist. A married bachelor does not exist. A fun Christian does not exist. (I made up the last one just to see if you're paying attention, but you can see the point.)

Next is the **Law of Noncontradiction**. You employ this law many times per day without even realizing it. This law holds that contradictory statements cannot both be true at the same time and in the same sense. Here is an example of a statement that is true: *A stationary object is not walking*. This fulfills the Law of Noncontradiction because there are no incompatible claims within the sentence. Here is an example of statement that is false: *I do not have time to write this sentence*. This violates the law of noncontradiction because the claim does not meet its own standard. You do not need any additional or independent information to know this sentence is false. It is simply a self-defeating statement.

The third of the "first principles" is the **Law of the Excluded Middle**. This law holds that any one thing is true or its negation is true. There is no third alternative. For example, you are either human or you are not human. A mile is either 5,280 feet, or a mile is not 5,280 feet. Murder is wrong, or murder is right. God exists, or God does not exist. Jesus rose from the dead, or Jesus did not rise from the dead. There are no third alternatives.

Are these principles obvious?

Yes.

Then why do we allow self-defeating statements to run rampant in the world?

We live in an age of skepticism, relativism, and pluralism. Collectively, this is called the "postmodern" era. There is a pervasive movement in our culture to regard all positions as true regardless of their correspondence to fact or reality. We live in a culture of catchy slogans rather than detailed, accurate facts. These slogans are repeated and touted as true despite that, oftentimes, many of these sound bites violate the first principles.

I have been guilty of this. You may have been guilty of this. We must practice identifying and refuting these self-defeating statements by using the first principles. Simply read the slogan, think, and apply the claim to itself to observe the falsehood.

Slogan: "There is no truth."

Refutation: If there is no truth, then the statement, "There is no truth" cannot itself be true. Therefore, that slogan is false.

Slogan: "There are no absolutes."

Refutation: If there are no absolutes, then the statement, "There are no absolutes" is not absolute. Therefore, that slogan is false.

Slogan: "Truth is relative."

Refutation: If truth is relative, then the statement, "Truth is relative" is also relative and does not apply to me right now. Therefore, that slogan is false.

Slogan: "Question everything."

Refutation: If I should question everything, then I should question the concept of questioning everything. Therefore, that slogan is false.

Slogan: "Anything is possible."

Refutation: If anything is possible, then the concept of impossibility is possible. Therefore, that slogan is false.

Slogan: "That might be true for you, but it's not true for me."

Refutation: Try the following exercise: Go to a car dealership and try to buy a Lamborghini with a personal check. When they verify the funds in your account, they will tell you that you do not have $275,000. Say to them, "That might be true for you, but it's not true for me." See how that works out for you.

Slogan: "Everything in moderation."

Refutation: If everything in moderation is true, then I should use moderation in moderation. Therefore, that slogan is false.

Do you see how all these statements violate the first principles? They are simply self-defeating claims because they cannot meet their own standards. You might think these statements are superfluous. You might think these statements are harmless. You might think that I am playing with words. Yes, logic can be fun, but it's also true.

There are dangerous self-defeating statements that are veiled under alleged virtues of fairness and tolerance. We have allowed these statements to be regarded as truth despite the fact that they violate the first principles. This is an alarming development. Again: read the slogan, think, and apply the claim to itself to observe the falsehood.

Slogan: "You can't really know anything."

Refutation: If I can't really know anything, then I can't know that statement is true. Therefore, that slogan is false.

Slogan: "We must not tolerate intolerance."

Refutation: If I should not tolerate intolerance, then I should not tolerate your intolerance of intolerance. Therefore, that statement is false. The claim itself is intolerant.

Slogan: "It's wrong to impose your views on others."

Refutation: That statement itself is a view that the speaker is attempting to impose on others. Do you see the violation of the Law of Noncontradiction?

Slogan: "All religions are the same."

Refutation: This is not necessarily a self-defeating claim. However, religions make contradictory truth claims; therefore, they are not the same and cannot all be true. Either Christianity is true, or Christianity is not true. There is no third alternative.

My personal favorite fallacious slogan is, "Don't judge."

Refutation: That statement itself is a judgment on judging. Therefore, the statement does not meet its own standard and is logically false. "Don't judge" is a judgment, so it violates the law of noncontradiction.

Here is an experiment: to the person who says, "Don't judge," say, "You look nice today." Or say, "You are very smart."

Will this person respond to you by saying, "Don't judge!" or, "Stop judging me!" or, "You shouldn't judge people!"? No, he will not say that because you are making a judgment that he agrees with. People only say, "Don't judge" if they do not agree with your judgment or they perceive the judgment to be negative. People never lecture you about "judging" if they agree with your judgment or think it's a positive statement. This behavior proves that people do not oppose the act of judging in and of itself; they simply oppose judgments that do not align with their own judgments!

You make judgments every day based on what you know is true. Throughout your entire life, you have judged whether a behavior is right or a behavior is wrong. You have passed these judgments on to your children. You judge that it is wrong to cross a busy street without looking both ways. You judge that certain foods are healthy and other foods are unhealthy, and the frequency of their consumption. Everyone makes behavior judgments many times every single day.

Let's shift back to absolute truth. Did you ever notice how we **demand** absolute truth from doctors, pharmacists, engineers, airplane pilots, inspectors, our boss, our spouse, and our children? We are appalled and offended when they don't give us absolute truth. Everyone mandates that certain people "tell the truth." But it seems that people try to evade the truth only when they are navigating the moral or religious arenas.[5] We will explore this phenomenon in a future chapter.

Using the first principles of logic, we have demonstrated that, yes, absolute truth does exist.

Which brings us to the next step in presenting a positive case that Christianity is true:

Does God exist?

A person who says, "Don't judge" is not only being hypocritical (illustrated above), but the statement is self-defeating, which means that it is false.

The statement exempts itself from its own standard because it is a judgment on judging.

CHAPTER 3

DOES GOD EXIST?
(USING THE BEGINNING OF THE UNIVERSE)

Have you ever "star-gazed"? Recall the last time you were removed from a major metropolitan area with minimal artificial light disturbance. Perhaps you were camping, on vacation, or at a cottage. You simply stared into the night sky in amazement. Taking in the immense universe, you were awestruck. My childhood vacation spot was Lake Summerset, Illinois, which is located about one hundred miles northwest of Chicago. After sunset, I laid on a lawn chair and glared at the vast expanse of substance that danced before me. I reached my hand up before my eyes and encircled a particular star into my fist. Upon relaxing my hand, the star would reappear as if I was releasing it back into the deep. I imagined: *This is the ease with which God created the universe.*

But how do we know God created the universe? That's what we will cover in this chapter.

The universe is the totality of space, matter, and time. For the purposes of this book, I will refer to space and matter as the material component of existence and time as the temporal component of existence. The sum combination of space, matter, and time is the universe. We can leverage the universe itself to prove the great probability that God exists.

In fact, the remainder of this chapter will address how to use the beginning of the universe (space, matter, and time) to demonstrate that, yes, God **does** exist.

Here is the logical presentation (this syllogism is referred to as the cosmological argument):

A) Everything that begins to exist has a cause.
B) The universe began to exist.
C) Therefore, the universe has a cause.

Examine the **A** premise. "Everything that **begins to exist** has a cause." Note the emphasis on the words "**begins to exist**." The contention is **NOT** simply, "Everything that exists has a cause," because that would imply that God himself requires a cause, which is not true. Rather, the contention is, "Everything that **begins to exist** has a cause."

This is known as the Law of Causality. Everything that has a beginning has a cause for its beginning. This premise is an undeniable law of the universe. Something cannot come from nothing. Zero plus zero is still zero. Being cannot arise from non-being. To deny the first premise is to deny all rational thought. If things that begin to exist do not have causes, then why doesn't a million dollars suddenly arise in front of you? Why doesn't a bear appear before you and maul you to death? The chair in which you are sitting was caused by a carpenter compiling wood or plastic into a static object in the shape of a chair. It was caused; it didn't suddenly begin to exist from nothing. The **A** premise is easy to defend; very few people legitimately try to deny it.

We have established the **A** premise based on obvious rationale. Let's move to the **B** premise: "The universe began to exist."

Let's think for a second. We know the universe currently exists. But did it **begin to** exist? I would be happy to admit that God does not exist if the universe didn't have a beginning because then it doesn't need a cause. It would just simply exist. But we know that the universe had a definite beginning. We know the universe is **not** infinite. The universe began to exist. Almost the entire scientific community agrees upon this fact, and here are just a few reasons why:

Uranium. Uranium is a radioactive element that decays into lead (another element) after billions of years.[6] If the universe has an age of infinity, then all uranium would already be lead. Billions of years are less than infinity; therefore, the amount of time it takes for uranium to turn into lead has already passed, so all uranium would already be lead. But it's not. We still have uranium, which means the universe is **not** eternal and had a definite beginning.

Black Dwarfs. To know what a black dwarf is, you must know what a white dwarf is. In very simple terms, a white dwarf is a compact star that has burned its nuclear fuel so that it starts to cool. A white dwarf is the final stage for most stars in the universe, including our sun. It takes several billion years for a star to devolve into a white dwarf. After a star becomes a white dwarf, it cools over the next several billion years to where it no longer emits light or heat and becomes a black dwarf. Yet no black dwarfs exist.[7] This means that the universe is not eternal, because if it were, then white dwarfs would have already turned into black dwarfs. The fact that no black dwarfs exist proves that the universe had an absolute beginning and is not infinite.

The Laws of Thermodynamics. The First Law of Thermodynamics states that the amount of energy in the universe is constant. There is a finite quantity of energy in the universe. The Second Law of Thermodynamics states that the amount of usable energy in the universe is decreasing.[8] The universe is running out of usable energy because it is consuming energy to "run."

Once you take your cell phone off the charger, it has a finite amount of energy. This is like the First Law of Thermodynamics. Now, as long as your cell phone is turned on, it is consuming energy to run. This is like the Second Law of Thermodynamics. If you took your phone off the charger an **infinite** time ago, your phone would be dead by now. The battery would have already run out of power. How long can your phone run on a full battery? Maybe a day or two, but it cannot run forever. It cannot run an infinite amount of time on a finite amount of energy. The same scientific fact applies to the universe. The universe has a finite amount of energy (first law), and since it is using energy to run (second law), it cannot run forever. If the universe were **infinite**, that means it has been running forever. If this were the case, then it would have already run out of energy because there is a fixed amount of usable energy in the universe (first law). But obviously, the universe has **not** run out of energy; therefore, the universe is not infinite. The universe had a definite beginning.

<u>The Radiation Afterglow</u>. Go to Holmdel, New Jersey, and see what Arno Penzias and Robert Wilson discovered in 1965. They won a Nobel Prize for discovering the cosmic microwave background radiation (or radiation afterglow). They used their instruments and antennas to detect the lingering heat from the initial explosion of the universe beginning to exist.[9] You can physically go to the observatory and see the radiation afterglow. Most of the atheists who supported the archaic "steady state" model of the infinite and eternal universe have seen the radiation afterglow or its data and cannot deny that the universe began to exist. They admit that the patterns of wavelengths undeniably originate from the "Big Bang." Yes, **that** Big Bang. As a Christian apologist, you need to embrace the Big Bang because it proves premise **B** of your argument: that the universe began to exist. When someone asks, "Do you believe in the Big Bang?" you respond in jest as Frank Turek does: "Yes, I just know who banged it."[10]

<u>Temporal Finitude</u>. Time is sequential. With each passing day, we add a day to time. But can you add anything to infinity? No. You cannot perform an addition operation to infinity. But since we can add another day to time (tomorrow), then time is not infinite.[11] Time is finite because we can add another thing to its sequence. Look at it this way: you cannot traverse an infinite set of days because you would never arrive at a fixed point.

Picture a bookshelf with an infinite number of books; there would be no "beginning" or "end" book on this shelf. If you selected a book at random, would you be able to assign a number to that book? **No**! You would have no fixed endpoints with which to reference (assign a number) to that book. Furthermore, no matter which book you selected, it would **not** be the "last" book in the sequence because there is no "last" in infinity. However, there is a "last" day to the present sequence in time (today); therefore, time is **not** infinite. Time is finite. Time itself began to exist.

Using these facts, you have proven that the universe began to exist. And everything that **begins to exist** has a cause. Therefore, the irrefutable conclusion is that the universe has a cause.

But what is this cause?

Based on the evidence provided in this argument, we can logically infer several facts about the nature of this cause. Since this agent **caused** the universe, it cannot be "of" the universe. It exists, by definition, independently of the universe. Therefore, this cause is immaterial (it is not made of materials). This cause is, at the point of creation, timeless (it exists independently of our notion of time). This cause is not confined to a spatial or material component; it is not confined to a temporal component (time). For these reasons, we know this cause has no limits. This cause is utterly powerful because it started the universe itself from no preexisting material. This cause is utterly intelligent because it started the universe with fine precision (this will be explained in the next chapter). This cause is personal because it made a **choice** to initiate the universe. This cause could have had other nothingness remain in perpetuity, but it **chose** to create the universe. Benign, impersonal objects do not make choices. A chair cannot make a choice. Mathematics cannot make choices. Only personal agents make choices; therefore, this cause is a personal agent because it made a choice to initiate the universe (space, matter, and time) from nothing.

On the following page you see a man holding a book.
He is presented with an "infinite bookshelf." There is no "first" or "last" book on the shelf.

If he were to place the book at any location on the shelf, what number book would it be? The fact is that you would not be able to assign it a number in an infinite set.

Conversely, we can assign a number to a moment of time (today is X).

Therefore, our present dimension of time cannot be infinite
and therefore had a definite beginning point,
which in turn, means time had a cause independent of itself.

We defined and presented the **cause** of the universe: a personal, immaterial, timeless (at the point of creation), limitless, powerful, personal, and intelligent being. What is the generic one-word name of this being?

God.

At this point the following objection might arise:

"Who made God?" or "What caused God?"

In some cases, these are honest questions. In other cases, "Who made God?" is a regurgitated slogan. Oftentimes, the objector has not even examined the truth of this catchphrase. Sometimes, people blurt out random objections. They move from one objection to the other without stopping to examine the truth. This is called "objection hopping." Later in this book, we will cover how to handle popular objections to Christianity. But let's kill one particular objection right now:

"Who made God?" or "What caused God?"

The word "made" implies a property of **matter**. The word "caused" implies a property of **time**. We just demonstrated how God exists independently of matter and time, so he cannot have those properties (at the point of creation). The question "Who made God?" commits a logical fallacy known as a **category mistake**. A category mistake is when someone tries to ascribe a property to something that cannot possibly possess that property. For example, it's like asking:

"What is the name of a bachelor's wife?" or "What does red taste like?"

The bachelor, by definition, cannot have the property of a wife. The color red, by definition, cannot have the property of taste. At the point of creation, God, by definition, cannot have the property of matter or the property of time that is implied by using the words "made" and "caused"; therefore, those are invalid questions. Very simply: God was not made. He could not have been made because He does not contain matter. God was not caused. He could not have been caused because He is not essentially limited to time. God is self-existent.

Another way to navigate the "Who made God?" objection is by the following illustration. A group of scientists arrive at a remote island in the middle of the ocean. This is the first known human contact with this island. No humans have ever been known to inhabit or visit this island. The scientists explore the island and discover pottery, tools, and remains of shelter. The scientists, knowing that these items can only be produced by intelligent beings, conclude that humans had been on the island. Even though the scientists cannot fully explain the humans, they still hold to the logical conclusion that humans produced the artifacts. It would be absurd to tell the scientists, "Humans on this island don't exist because you can't explain them." That's nonsense. The scientists would present the evidence (artifacts) and point to the best logical conclusion (humans existed on the island). Likewise, the "Who made God?" objection does not prove God doesn't exist. Just because we cannot fully explain everything about God does not mean He doesn't exist. We look at the evidence (i.e. the beginning of the universe and other evidence in the following chapters) and point to the best logical conclusion (God does exist).[12]

By using the law of causality, coupled with the scientific fact of the definite beginning of the universe, you have proven the need for an independent first cause of the universe. Based on the inferences drawn from this argument, you have demonstrated that, yes, God does exist.

In the next chapter, we will explore another line of reasoning called the "classical argument" and how it answers the question:

Does God exist?

DOES GOD EXIST?
(USING THE UNIVERSE ITSELF)

Imagine a time when nothing exists. Literally nothing. I am misleading you a little bit, because by inviting you to imagine something, then by definition, you are **not** truly imagining **nothing**. Something is not nothing. Also, I am misleading you by saying, "Imagine a **time** when nothing exists." Time itself is something, so it is impossible to imagine a "time" when nothing existed.

That being said, give it your best shot. Imagine a time when nothing exists. Literally nothing. No time. No space. No matter. No land. No sea. No air. No earth. No sky. No sun. No stars. No galaxies. No universe. No God. **No <u>thing</u>**. **Nothing**. Absolute nothingness.

If there was a time when nothing existed, how could anything exist?

It couldn't.

Something cannot come from nothing. Out of nothing, nothing comes. Every effect has an antecedent cause. This is the Law of Causality that we covered in Chapter 3. We see effects all around us. Time. Space. Matter. Land. Sea. Air. Earth. Sky. Sun. Stars. Galaxies. The universe itself is an effect; therefore, it requires an antecedent cause apart from itself. If literally nothing existed before the universe, then there would be nothing to cause it to be an effect. It would not exist.

But since it does exist, there must be a cause. There must be a cause with the power of being in and of itself. There must be a self-existent eternal entity responsible for the effects.

The following paragraph is worth repeating: We can logically infer several facts about the nature of this entity. Since this agent **caused** the universe, it cannot be "of" the universe. It exists, by definition, independently of the universe. Therefore, this cause is immaterial (it is not made of materials). This cause is timeless (it exists independent of our notion of time). This cause is not confined to a spatial or material component; it is not confined to a temporal component (time). For these reasons, we know this cause has no limits. This cause is utterly powerful because it started the universe itself from no preexisting material. This cause is personal because it made a **choice** to initiate the universe. This cause could have had other nothingness remain in perpetuity, but it **chose** to create the universe. Benign, impersonal objects do not make choices. A chair cannot make a choice. Mathematics cannot make choices. Only personal agents make choices; therefore, this cause is a personal agent because it made a choice to initiate the universe (space, matter, and time) from nothing.

We defined and presented the cause of the universe: a personal, immaterial, timeless (at the point of creation), limitless, powerful, and intelligent being. What is the generic one-word name of this being?

God.

The current fact that something exists proves that nothingness was impossible. By coupling this fact with the Law of Causality, you have established the need for an independent first cause of the universe. Based on the inferences drawn from this argument, you have demonstrated that, yes, God does exist.

*Although this is not a perfect analogy, you can think of a necessary being by using the above illustration. If the tree roots and trunk did not exist, then the leaves and fruit **could not** exist. It would be impossible. Likewise, if a necessary being did not exist, then nothing could exist because out of nothing, nothing comes.*

In the next chapter, we will explore another line of reasoning called the "fine-tuning of the universe" and how it answers the question:

Does God exist?

CHAPTER 4

DOES GOD EXIST?
(USING THE FINE-TUNING OF THE UNIVERSE)

Visualize the classic safety pin. To the naked eye, it consists of a fairly simple spring mechanism and a clasp. A safety pin seems to be a simple piece of metal with a twist at the bend and a point at the end. The pointy end is inserted into an opening (clasp) so that it doesn't puncture anything; hence, the term "safety" pin. Although it is a relatively simple machine, if all the components are not simultaneously present and/or not functioning with precision, the safety pin does not work. If the spring mechanism (twisty part) does not hold the proper amount of tension, the pointy part of the pin will be too tight or too loose and will not fit into the clasp. If the clasp itself is too wide or too narrow, the pointy part will not fit. If the metal is too long or too short, the safety pin will not work. The safety pin is fine-tuned so that it will serve its purpose (fasten clothing, etc.) **only** if the fine-tuning is present.

If you were walking down the street and found a safety pin, would you assume it was randomly constructed by random chance? Did the wind and dust amalgamate into a safety pin by random chance? Or, did the safety pin have a designer? Which is the better conclusion?

The universe is an extremely complex machine that requires all of its parts to be functioning with precision to work. The universe is fine-tuned so that **life** can exist. Are we to believe that the universe came into being by random chance? That seems absurd to me. If a mere safety pin cannot be produced by random chance, then an exponentially more complex machine such as the universe cannot be produced by random chance. The fine-tuning of the universe points to a designer. The remainder of this chapter will address how to use the fine-tuning of the universe to demonstrate that, yes, God **does** exist.

Let's examine the fine-tuning of the universe. The universe is specifically fine-tuned to permit life. There are dozens of inter-reliant and meticulous circumstances present in the universe that enable life to exist. These extremely precise and interactive conditions are known as the "anthropic constants." The anthropic constants are a series of mutually interdependent configurations existing in the universe that can be identified and measured; therefore, they constitute a body of empirical evidence proving a highly complex fine-tuning of the universe. There are over 122 anthropic constants. We will explore a few of them here:

There are four fundamental forces of the universe: gravity, electromagnetism, and the strong and weak nuclear forces.

Each planet has its own gravitational force, and this is an anthropic constant. If this force was adjusted by even 0.000000000000000000000000000000000 0001 percent, then the stars would not exist in their present locations.[13]

If the strong nuclear force were a fraction of a percentage stronger (roughly 0.3 percent), then protons and neutrons would be so forceful that specific types of protons would be so rare that hydrogen atoms would not exist.[14]

Gravity is 10^{39} times weaker than electromagnetism.[15] Decrease that ratio to 10^{33} and the stars would burn out a million times faster.

At the point of the beginning of the universe, if the delta between the strong nuclear force and electromagnetism had been off by 1 in 100,000,000,000,000,000, then no stars would have formed.[16]

There are over 200 billion stars in the Milky Way galaxy. The average distance between those stars is 30 trillion miles.[17] Try to comprehend that distance. Thirty trillion miles! The New Horizons spacecraft travels at 36,373 miles per hour. That's ten miles per **second**! At the point of its launch, it was the fastest man-made object on a trajectory away from earth. It would take the New Horizons spacecraft **94,154 years** to travel between just one single star to another single star in our galaxy. Why is this important? Because the average distance between those stars (30 trillion miles) is an anthropic constant. If that distance was altered, then planetary momentum would be affected. Planetary momentum is another anthropic constant. If the centrifugal force of planetary movement did not perfectly counterbalance gravitational force, then celestial bodies could orbit around one another.

Another finely tuned anthropic constant is the expansion rate of the universe. If the universe expands at a rate of one-millionth of a unit faster, then the universe would collapse.[18]

Another anthropic constant is the planet Jupiter. Jupiter is like a magnetic garbage dump in outer space. There is a crater on Jupiter the size of the Pacific Ocean caused by an asteroid the size of the Titanic. Due to the exact size, exact gravitational field, exact number of moons, and exact orbit of Jupiter, it attracts asteroids and comets that, without Jupiter, would inevitably crash into earth.[19]

The seasonal 23° tilt of the earth is fine-tuned. If the earth were tilted at a significantly higher or lower degree, then one of the hemispheres would be too close to the sun and burn up. The other hemisphere would be too far from the sun and freeze over. This is an anthropic constant. So is the fact that the rotation of the earth is precisely 23 hours, 56 minutes, and 4 seconds. If that time were significantly faster, the temperature delta between day and night would be too extreme to enable life.[20]

The oxygen level on earth is an anthropic constant. The atmosphere is built with 21 percent oxygen. If it were significantly higher, there would be erratic explosions. If the oxygen level were several percentage points lower, we would asphyxiate.[21]

Have you ever been to the beach and noticed the water level being different than the last time you were there? You witnessed another anthropic constant. The gravitational interaction between the moon and the earth is so precise that if it were significantly modified, then the tidal forces would cause a climatic cataclysm where the earth could be flooded.[22] (Sound familiar?)

Even seemingly destructive forces such as lightning and earthquakes are anthropic constants. If there were much more frequent lightning, then more wildfires would ignite across the earth. But, if there were much less lightning, then there would be a nitrogen deficiency in the soil so plants would not grow. If there was a significant increase in earthquakes, then more man-made structures would be destroyed. But, if there was significantly less seismic activity, then nutrients on ocean floors and riverbeds would not be recycled back to the landmass.[23]

There are more than 122 anthropic constants currently known to man. If any of these constants were altered, then a life-permitting universe would cease to exist and would have never existed in the first place. The conditions of the universe are fine-tuned with precision.

But **why** is the universe fine-tuned?

There are three options: Necessity, random chance, or a designer.

Necessity. This option posits that the quantities present in the fine-tuning of the universe are physically necessary. This option is not true. The quantities of the anthropic constants are not physically necessary. In fact, even Stephen Hawking, an atheist physicist, says that the measures of the constants could have **any** values![24] Even the most advanced physical theories cannot predict that the exact quantities of the fine-tuning would be what they are. Therefore, we can rule out physical necessity as the reason why the universe is fine-tuned.

Random chance. The first note about random chance is that chance itself is not a **cause**. Chance is simply a mathematical description we use in regard to probability. Chance has zero causal prowess unto itself.[26] So even if chance could be the explanation for the fine-tuning, chance cannot produce the anthropic constants themselves, such as gravity. This being noted, let's leave that to the side and see if chance is the best explanation for the fine-tuning of the universe.

We have seen that the anthropic constants are fine-tuned so that this life-permitting universe exists. What is the probability that all of this fine-tuning is due to random chance? Not good. That's my answer. Here is the mathematical answer: **1 in 10^{138}**. I repeat: The probability of a life-permitting universe existing by random chance is **1 in 10^{138}** (that is 10 with 138 zeros after it!).[25] You can barely even fathom the size of that number. Try to put it in your calculator right now. You'll probably receive an error that indicates the magnitude of that number. It's almost incomprehensible. You can try to visualize it this way:

Have you ever entered a raffle? Imagine the kind of raffle where the administrator has a roll of one trillion perforated tickets, tears one off, and gives it to you. Then, all of the corresponding tickets are stacked up and one will be selected. Picture that type of raffle but with one caveat. Every single ticket has the number five written on it—except for your ticket. Your ticket is the only one out of the trillion that has the number six written on it.

Okay. Now, the height of this stack of one trillion tickets is **67,866 miles** high![27] This would stretch one-fourth of the way to the moon! What is the probability of your ticket being selected by random chance? Not good. That's my answer. Here is the mathematical answer: one in one trillion. That is 1 in 10^{12}. Do you see how improbable it is for your ticket to be selected by random chance? Actually, in comparison to the universe, you might want to enter the raffle. The probability of the universe existing by random chance is **1 in 10^{138}**, which is exponentially **less** likely than your ticket being picked in the raffle!

Due to the overwhelmingly low (next to utterly impossible) odds of winning the raffle, if your ticket was selected, you would rightly think that the raffle was **not** a product of random chance, but rather the raffle was a product of a designer. You would assume someone rigged it. In the same manner, you can see the complex fine-tuning of the universe and rightly think that someone rigged it—and that "someone" doing the rigging is known as a designer.

The fine-tuning of the universe is a product of a designer. We know this already because we ruled out physical necessity and random chance based on sheer improbability (effectively zero). We also have positive evidence that the universe is a product of a designer. When you see objects that are fine-tuned, you almost always infer a designer. For example, when you see a painting on a wall, you can safely assert a painter. When you see a clock on a wall, you can safely assert a clockmaker. When you see a building, you can safely assert an architect (designer). Things that are fine-tuned don't randomly spring into existence by random chance. They are a product of a designer. Even a relatively simple fine-tuned item such as a safety pin is designed. It stands to reason that an incredibly complex system like the universe must also be the product of design.

Based on the evidence provided in this argument, we can logically infer several facts about the nature of this designer. Since this agent designed the universe, it cannot be "of" the universe. It exists, by definition, independently of the universe. Think of it this way: The painter is independent of his painting. The clockmaker is independent of his clock. The architect is independent of the building he designs. We can learn certain characteristics of the painter by his painting, but the painter exists externally from the painting. Likewise, we can learn certain characteristics of the designer by his design (the universe), but the designer exists externally from the universe. Therefore, this designer is immaterial (it is not made of materials), nor is the designer confined to space. For these reasons, we know this designer has no physical limits. This designer is absolutely intelligent because it designed the universe with this incomprehensible fine-tuning.

We defined and presented the **designer** of the universe: an immaterial, spaceless, limitless, and intelligent being. What is the generic one-word name of this being?

God.

By using the fine-tuning of the universe, you have proven beyond a reasonable doubt (1 in 10^{138}) that the universe is a product of a designer. Using the inferences drawn from this argument, you have demonstrated that, yes, God does exist.

In the next chapter we will explore another line of reasoning called the "message contained in life" and how it can help to answer the question:

Does God exist?

The standard safety pin is a relatively simple fine-tuned machine.
There is no doubt that it is the product of a designer.

The universe is an exponentially more complex fine-tuned machine.
Therefore, it is reasonable to conclude that the universe is also the product of a designer.

CHAPTER 5

DOES GOD EXIST?
(USING THE MESSAGE CONTAINED IN LIFE)

Imagine you are walking down the sidewalk. You come across a crack in the concrete. You see the block of cement and a simple gash is running through it. What is the most probable cause of the crack in the sidewalk? The answer is **natural forces**. This little fissure in the concrete is a product of erosion, freeze-thaw action, water damage, or basic entropy—otherwise referred to as **natural forces**. You can safely assume that natural forces caused the crack in the sidewalk. You don't even think twice about it.

Now, imagine you are walking down the sidewalk. This time you come across something that is slightly similar to a crack in the concrete. This time, the gashes in the sidewalk spell out the words "I LOVE YOU." The letters I, L, O, V, E, Y, O, and U are organized in the precise arrangement to form the message: "I LOVE YOU."

What is the most probable cause of this imprint in the sidewalk? Should you assume it was caused by natural forces? The other crack in the sidewalk was caused by natural forces, so should you think that erosion and entropy caused the words "I LOVE YOU" to appear in the sidewalk? Maybe by random chance several inert cracks correctly ordered themselves to form the words "I LOVE YOU."

What is the best explanation for the imprint in each sidewalk?
Natural forces or an intelligent agent?

What? That seems absurd to me. The true cause of the words in the sidewalk is that a person with an intelligent mind dipped his finger in the wet cement and then it dried, so the words were embossed in the concrete. The inscription "I LOVE YOU" is a **message**. Unlike the benign crack in the first example, the engraving of "I LOVE YOU" communicates direct information in an organized system of characters. Natural forces cannot produce a **message** in this manner, and it's almost impossible for random chance to produce a **message**.

The only entity known to produce a message is an intelligent mind.

Similar to the message "I LOVE YOU" in the sidewalk, every single living cell on earth has a specifically arranged set of characters that expresses a direct message. This message is communicated in DNA. Because life contains extremely complex messages, it cannot be a product of natural forces or random chance (or any combination). Life is a product of an intelligent mind. The remainder of this chapter will address how to use the message contained in life to help demonstrate that, yes, God does exist.

Let's examine the message contained in DNA.

DNA (deoxyribonucleic acid) is a molecule that is present and essential in every living cell of every form of life. The purpose of DNA is to encode a message that instructs other components to perform a specific function or complete a specific task. To understand how this process works, you need to have a fundamental grasp of the actual structure of DNA.

The complete structure of DNA is astonishingly complex. Just ask any molecular biologist or search the Internet for an animated demonstration. The basic overview is that two opposing strands coil around each other to form a double helix. There are nitrogen bases connected all up and down the strands. The nitrogen bases are the "rungs." There are four separate bases—either guanine (G), adenine (A), thymine (T), or cytosine (C).[27] Using an overly simplified analogy, you can think of the composition of DNA like a twisted ladder. Each rung of the ladder has letters written on it, forming a specific combination of either G, A, T, or C. This is where we will focus on the information in DNA and how it expresses a message.

The modern alphabet has twenty-six letters. The letters themselves are considered "information." You can randomly type letters, and at best, you have information. But, take it one step further—if you arrange this information

41

(the letters) in a specific order, you can rightly convey a message. Intelligent minds are the only entities that can produce a message. Likewise, the DNA "alphabet" has four letters (G, A, T, or C on the rungs). The letters themselves are information. If random letters were compiled together within DNA, life would not function. However, the letters are arranged in a very precise order to express a message. This message is issued to other biological units to perform a specific function to enable life. The only entity capable of this process is an intelligent mind, not natural causes or random chance.

How much information are we talking about? Even a single-cell organism such as an amoeba has a staggering amount of information. If you typed out all of the G's, A's, T's, and C's in the DNA of an amoeba, you would have over one thousand phone books for twenty-five different cities![28] And that is just for a single-cell organism. Note that this information is not randomly typed out; it is sequenced with absolute precision (just like the letters in a phone book) to express a message.

To put this in perspective, remember: assemblies of DNA transmit messages and some cells contain millions of DNA packages. Using the ladder analogy, there are certain cells that contain about 6,000,000,000 (6 billion) rungs of nitrogen bases. If those rungs were separated by an equal distance as rungs on a standard ladder, the ladder would reach halfway to the moon! That is just one cell! And the human body has an estimated 37,000,000,000,000 (37 trillion) cells, each of which can contain billions of rungs![29] It's almost impossible to comprehend the number of messages being expressed in the cells of a human being.

There is even more complexity contained in all the machinery required to build the units and program the messages. Additionally, there is yet another layer of complexity contained in the biological structures and mechanisms required to decode, decipher, interpret, and deliver the messages.[30]

Back to the main question: can natural forces or random chance store information in a precise order to communicate a message? The answer is **NO**. Here is the final demonstration I will give you to reinforce this fact.

Do you remember those multicolored magnetic refrigerator letters? Maybe you have a child and you have those magnetic letters on your refrigerator right now. Suppose you wake up one morning and walk into your kitchen. You see all of the letters scattered about the face of the fridge in no specific arrangement. They are randomly spread around. You would not think anything of it. Obviously, the letters were simply placed on the refrigerator at random.

Now, suppose you wake up one morning and walk into your kitchen. This time, the letters are specifically ordered to form the words "I LOVE YOU." Should you assume that someone blindly put his hand in the container and randomly spread the letters in this sequence by pure random chance? Should you assume that an electrical surge made the refrigerator rumble and the letters scrambled into this precise pattern by an unguided process (natural forces)? That seems absurd to me! Even though you didn't see a person do it, you know that someone arranged this information into an exact, specific order to communicate a **message**. It cannot be a product of natural forces or random chance. It can only be a product of an intelligent mind.

In the same manner, there is a message expressed in all living things that is unequivocally witnessed in DNA. By using this message, we have demonstrated that life is not a product of random chance or natural forces because those things cannot issue messages. The only entity capable of issuing a message is an intelligent mind.

What is the best explanation for the arrangement of letters on each refrigerator?
Natural forces, random chance, or an intelligent agent?

Based on the evidence provided in this argument, we can logically infer several facts about the nature of this intelligent mind. Since this agent produced the message contained in life, it must have free will. This agent could have gone on without communicating this message in life forms. This agent made a **choice** to create something. Only personal agents make choices. For example, a chair cannot make a choice. A force cannot make a choice. Again, only personal agents can make choices; therefore, this intelligent mind is **personal**. Also, due to the vast complexity of the message contained in life, we can assert that this mind is astoundingly **intelligent**. To set every single one of the trillions of characters into the precise arrangement to enable life requires intelligence that supersedes anything we have witnessed in this universe.

By using the message contained in human life combined with other evidence in this book, you can demonstrate that, yes, God does exist.

In the next chapter, we will explore another line of reasoning called the argument from "objective moral laws" and how it can answer the question:

Does God exist?

CHAPTER 6

DOES GOD EXIST?
(USING OBJECTIVE MORAL LAWS)

The Nazis performed human experiments on almost 1,500 sets of twin children. That's nearly three thousand children who were tortured for, according to the Nazis, the "greater good of humanity." One of the most harrowing experiments was performed by Josef Mengele. The "Angel of Death," as he was called, identified a set of twins, amputated their arms, and attempted to sew the two bodies together in an effort to create conjoined twins. Mengele conducted another experiment where he purposely injected a child with malaria mucous from a mosquito. He administered several different chemical compounds in an effort to discover a viable treatment.[31] His reason for this behavior was to help the greatest number of people flourish by developing a "cure" for various human defects.

Almost everyone knows that these experiments were wrong. These experiments highlight what I mean by "objective moral laws." An action is right, or it is wrong. In this book, I will use terms such as "right" and "wrong." I am using these terms in the context of the moral law illuminated by the Nazi experiments: what the Nazis did was, and always will be, wrong.

I have never personally encountered someone who truly thinks that what the Nazis did was right. It's fairly easy to demonstrate that objective moral laws exist by simply providing the stories of their experiments. Almost everyone will agree that what they did was, and always will be, wrong. If a person admits this, then he has effectively agreed that objective moral laws exist. Again, almost everyone falls into this category and admits some moral laws exist.

Now, the real point of contention is **what is the foundation of moral laws**?

The remainder of this chapter will address how to use objective moral laws to demonstrate that, yes, God *does* exist.

What is the foundation of moral laws? There are several different proposals that either fall under the **subjective** category or the **objective** category. We will explore six of the most common submissions in this chapter.

But first, we must define the meaning of an objective law. An objective law is one that is valid and binding regardless of human involvement. For example: 2+2=4. This is an objective mathematical law. Just imagine if every human on earth attended a meeting and decided that 2+2=5. Would the laws of mathematics change based on this vote? No. 2+2=4 regardless of human intervention.

Another criteria to define an objective law is that it is true for all people at all times and in all places. 2+2=4 will always be true and has always been true even before the first math textbook was written. This is another important distinction to fully comprehend: the difference between *how you know* something is true versus *why* something is true. The fancy term for *how you know* something is true is "epistemology." The fancy term for *why* something is true is "ontology."

To provide an illustration, try to remember who taught you that 2+2=4. Was it your parents? Maybe it was one of your elementary school teachers? It was probably a combination. My first grade teacher, Ms. Stesyk, taught me that 2+2=4. My parents reinforced that law through homework and so forth. This is epistemology. This is *how I know* that 2+2=4.

Now, imagine if I lived my entire life on an uninhabited island. Ms. Stesyk and my parents did not teach me that 2+2=4. No one did. Is it still true that 2+2=4, even though no one taught it to me? Yes, because it is an **objective** law. An objective law is true for all people at all times and in all places regardless of if or how someone knows it. Exploring *why a law is true* is called **ontology**. The discussion of "What is the foundation of moral laws?" is an exercise in **ontology**, not epistemology. We are talking about **why** a moral law is true (**not** *how we know* it is true). This distinction will become clearer as you read the remainder of this chapter.

Now that we have defined our terms and understood the difference between epistemology (**how** *you know something is true*) versus ontology (**why** *something is true*), we can examine the specific proposals:

A	The Foundation for Moral Laws is Subjective	B	The Foundation for Moral Laws is Objective
A1	Moral laws are a matter of personal preference. (You like chocolate; I like vanilla.)	B1*	The foundation of moral laws is to achieve the most human flourishing for the greatest number of people or to avoid the worst possible suffering for the greatest number of people.
A2	Societal conventions and laws dictate moral laws. (You should drive on the right side of the road, not the left side of the road.)	B2*	Evolution has ingrained moral laws into humans through a process of natural selection.
A3	Something is morally wrong only if it hurts someone else.	B3*	God is the foundation of moral laws.

*indicates the position is objective only by disguise; the argument is actually subjective.

Moral laws are definitely objective. Moral laws, similar to mathematical laws, are valid and binding regardless of human involvement. How can we demonstrate this? Imagine if the Nazis succeeded in their mission and conquered the entire world. Then, they proceeded to brainwash everyone into believing that their human experiments on children were morally right because they were trying to achieve a greater good for humanity. In the mind of the **subjects** (everyone on earth), the Nazis were doing something morally right. So now, are the Nazis morally right? **NO!** Even if every single person believed that the Nazis were right, they would still be morally wrong.[32] This means that the Nazi human experiments are **objectively** morally wrong regardless of human intervention. The following statement is true at all times and in all places: performing murderous experiments on children is wrong. This is a valid and binding moral law. By using this illustration, we can demonstrate that moral laws are **objective**.

Even though we demonstrated that moral laws are objective, thereby discarding any proposal in column *A*, for the sake of being thorough, we will briefly refute *A1*, *A2*, and *A3*.

A1: Moral laws are a matter of personal preference. (You like chocolate; I like vanilla.) This statement is obviously false. Did you ever encounter a bully on a playground? His personal preference was to steal your lunch money. If moral laws were a matter of taste, then he could not be punished for stealing your lunch money. He would not be "wrong" for doing so because he was only acting on his personal preference. This one is fairly obvious, but remember it for future reference.

A2: Societal conventions and laws dictate moral laws. (You should drive on the right side of the road, not the left side of the road.) Are moral laws simply dictated by society? If the government says something is permissible, then is it morally right? No. We've already seen the Nazi example. The Nazi government thought it was right to perform experiments on children, but that action is clearly morally wrong. The United States government repeatedly said it was right to own a slave against his/her will, but that action is morally wrong. These examples prove that moral laws are not simply founded on societal conventions.[33]

A3: Something is morally wrong only if it hurts someone else. If this were true, then drug addicts, pornographers, and prostitutes are not doing anything wrong. Their behavior is not directly harming anyone else; therefore, all of their actions are not wrong. As you can see, once you provide these examples, it becomes clear that the standard of right versus wrong does not hinge solely on the harm done to someone else. Here is another illustration: Imagine you have been waiting in line for twenty minutes to check out at the grocery store. Just when it is your turn to transact your business, someone cuts in front of you in line. You might be filled with rage. But, at the same exact moment, the adjacent cashier opens her register and invites you over to her. You complete your transaction in the same amount of time. No one was hurt. Did the line-cutter do something wrong? **Yes!** Even though he did not harm you, he still committed an action that is morally wrong. A behavior can be wrong even though it does not hurt another person.

Let's move to column *B*. These foundations are considered "objective" bases for moral laws.

B1*: The foundation of moral laws is to achieve the most human flourishing for the greatest number of people or to avoid the worst possible suffering for the greatest number of people. Please note the asterisk; the reason for the asterisk is because once we dissect this position, we quickly realize that it is a **subjective** foundation; it is **not** objective. That is because every individual person (a subject) must define the word "flourishing." Human "flourishing" means different things for different humans. For example, the Korowai people of Indonesian New Guinea currently practice cannibalism. They believe that this practice ensures human flourishing. When someone is convicted of sorcery or black magic, they believe that the person himself no longer exists. They believe that a demon has already killed him. The demon, literally, is now the person—flesh, bones, etc. Therefore, they kill it and eat it. According to them, they are **not** killing and eating their fellow tribesman; it is the demon they consume. Sometimes (perhaps the majority of the time) the "victim" is a willing participant in being eaten. The reason the community (including the "victim") does this act is for the flourishing of the majority of the tribe. They do not want the demon to kill other people. They believe that the only way to completely eradicate the demon is to eat him. In the minds of the Korowai, they do this to protect people. This example demonstrates how the word "flourishing" is subjective.

Here is another illustration of how achieving the most human "flourishing" for the greatest number of people is not a valid foundation for moral laws: a doctor identifies three patients who need organ transplants. One needs a heart, another needs a kidney, and another needs a pancreas. I am a viable candidate with healthy organs. The doctor would be morally right in killing me (one person) to acquire my organs to ensure the flourishing of the greater number of people (three).

These analogies might seem like extreme examples, but they effectively highlight the fallacy of *B1*. Words like "flourishing" and "suffering" are subjective.

Here is another, less extreme example: some people think skydiving is exhilarating and flourish from it. I, on the other hand, find misery in skydiving. Therefore, achieving the most human flourishing and avoiding the worst possible suffering are simply a matter of personal preference (subjective). In discussing *A1* we've already seen how personal preference is not a valid foundation for moral laws.

B2*: Evolution has ingrained moral laws into humans through a process of natural selection. We will diligently cover the topic of evolution in a future chapter. But for our present purposes, the argument in *B2* asserts that humans know how to act rightly because many generations of evolution have ingrained those instincts into us. Firstly, we must revisit the difference between epistemology and ontology. Even if this claim (*B2*) is true, evolution is how humans know right versus wrong; evolution does not tell you *why* something is right or wrong.[34] For example, the bully on the playground can steal your lunch money and argue that he has not "evolved" to the point of knowing theft is wrong. Therefore, it is not objectively wrong to steal lunch money. Theft is subjective based on an individual's stage of evolution. That is why you will notice the asterisk by *B2*. Evolution is a subjective foundation; it is not objective.

Furthermore, evolution posits that survival is the ultimate driving force of whether or not traits continue to endure. In other words, if evolution is the foundation of moral laws, then it would be morally right to perform an action if that action enables the survival of your species. Survival is the reason that the male spider monkey will forcibly copulate with his female counterpart. Evolution states that the monkey is simply trying to perpetuate his species; therefore, he has done nothing wrong. So why is the human rapist wrong? The rapist is not simply trying to ensure the survival of his genes. Obviously, rape is morally wrong, so *B2* is invalid.

Here is another illustration of why evolution is not the foundation of moral laws: Imagine you are waiting at a bus stop in the blistering cold. A stranger is standing next to you. Both of you have been waiting for thirty minutes. You are lucky to be wearing two pairs of gloves. The stranger is not wearing any gloves. In fact, he mutters, "I think my hands are getting frostbite." Will you give him your extra pair of gloves? If evolution dictates right and wrong, it would be wrong of you to give him your extra gloves because survival is the central tenet of evolution, and giving him your extra gloves does not increase your chances of survival. But, in spite of this, you know that giving him your extra gloves would be morally right. Using these examples, we can see how evolution is not the foundation of moral laws.

B1 and B2: Fittingly, the Nazis tried to combine these two positions to justify their behavior. The Nazis claimed that they were morally right by performing experiments on children because they were trying to achieve ultimate human flourishing by discovering cures for disease and researching generational defects. They said these heinous acts were morally right because the subjects were genetically disadvantaged; therefore, the Nazis asserted that they were simply aiding and assisting the evolutionary process.[35] Again, almost no one will argue that what the Nazis did was right. What they did provides us real-life examples of how objective morals laws exist and how claims to "flourishing" and evolution cannot be the foundation of those moral laws.

We have proven that moral laws exist. We have proven that all subjective foundations for moral laws are false. We have also demonstrated how the purported "objective" foundations of collective flourishing and evolution are actually subjective and also false. Therefore, the only alternative is that the foundation for moral law is objective.

But how does this prove that God is the foundation of moral laws?

God is the objective foundation for moral laws. The first method to prove this fact is by the process of elimination defined in the chart located in this chapter. By demonstrating that all other proposed foundations for moral laws are false, we can effectively point to God as the only viable alternative. That being said, we can also present a positive case in addition to the process of elimination.

Every command implies a commander. Every law implies a law-*giver*. Laws do not appear spontaneously out of thin air. Every law has a body (legislature) or a person who enacts the law. Moral laws are no different. Moral laws require a "person" to deliver them. This "person" (being) is God. God's very own nature— love, justice, grace, etc.—are the attributes on which moral laws are founded. Since God is unchanging and immutable, these attributes constitute an eternal, pure, and fixed foundation from which God can issue laws that dictate whether a behavior is right or wrong. God is the **object** in **object**ive law. As we have demonstrated in the previous chapters, God exists independently of our universe, so He is not swayed by the influences of time and space. The only objective moral law-giver can be God.

A common objection to the argument that God is the foundation of moral laws is, "I don't believe in God, but I am a good person." Or, "I don't need God to tell me how to be a good person."

Allow me to clarify the contention of this chapter right now. We don't necessarily need to believe in God to act rightly. Perhaps we have been taught the right objective moral laws, just as we have been taught that 2+2=4. We are not discussing *how* we know an action is right (epistemology). We are concerned with *why* an action is right (ontology). *Why* does someone think he is a "good person"? What is the foundation of that assessment? As we have seen in this chapter, the only possible objective foundation is God.

Usually, a person who says, "I am a good person," will base this statement on comparison. That is, they will provide an example of what is "good" only in relation to another person. This is a fool's errand. The drug addict can say, "I am a good person because I don't *deal* drugs." The drug dealer can say, "I am a good person because I don't *steal*." The thief can say, "I am a good person because I don't *murder*." The murderer can say, "I am a good person because I don't *rape*." The rapist can say, "At least I am not Hitler." As you can see, with this line of thinking, you can descend down the rubbish chute, and as long as you're not Hitler, you're a "good" person. This is moral relativism. This is subjectivism. This is false. The truth is that we have an unchanging measure of right and wrong. Yes, we have an objective standard of good. We have an immutable foundation for moral laws—God.

This illustration displays the logical conclusion to regarding morality as subjective. Everyone can justify himself as "right" in relation to someone else until you arrive at Hitler, who then can justify himself by claiming to be "right" by ensuring the most flourishing for the greatest number of people who, in his subjective opinion, deserve it.

Another common objection to the contention that God is the foundation of moral laws is, "If God is the foundation of moral laws, then why do so many Christians commit actions that are wrong?"

This claim appeals to what I refer to as the "Christian atrocity" objection. We will diligently cover this topic in a later chapter. But for the purposes of this chapter, we simply have to point out that as with any other truth claim, we must test the truth of Christianity based on the evidence, not on the actions of its constituents. Imagine that your first grade teacher was heinous. She committed wrong actions on a daily basis. She also told you that 2+2=4. Would you think that this arithmetic is false just because she is misbehaving? **No!** You would seek out the truth of her claim and test it for yourself. This is exactly what an objector should do with Christianity. Seek the truth; don't blindly dismiss it because a person who claims to be Christian has done something wrong.

Furthermore, ironically, if Christianity is true, then Christians doing "wrong" is exactly what we should expect. Christianity teaches that everyone falls short of the objective moral standard of God. Even Christians. We will cover this in detail in a future chapter.

By presenting the existence of objective moral laws and that God is the foundation of those laws, we have demonstrated that, yes, God does exist. We now have four separate lines of reasoning leading to the overwhelming probable conclusion that yes, God does exist.

In the next chapter, we will explore the answer to the following question:

Are miracles possible?

CHAPTER 7

ARE MIRACLES POSSIBLE?

Do you have a home computer? Do you have a work computer? Do you need a username and password to log in to one of those computers? Think about your computer, which requires your credentials. In order to access this computer, you need authorization. Once you have proven your authorization, you can install new programs, add new functionality, and upload new data into your computer. You have the **author**ity to feed new events into the system.

As we have thoroughly explored in previous chapters, God is the **author** of the universe. Therefore, he has the **author**ity to feed new events into the system. These new events are sometimes called miracles. Very simply, a miracle is an event that cannot be explained by natural laws. Since God instituted those natural laws, he can create occurrences that are not bound by them.

Think about the laws of your household. You make the kids go to bed at 9 p.m. But on rare occasions, you allow them to "violate" the law by staying awake later than 9 p.m. Since you enacted the laws, you can create new situations that are not bound by them. Likewise, since God created the universe and the laws that govern it, He can introduce a new event into the system, an event which is not bound by natural laws (a miracle).[36]

It is very important to first answer, "Does God exist?" By using the lines of reasoning in the previous chapters, we can demonstrate that, yes, God does exist. After that, the argument to affirm miracles is actually fairly simple.

First, let's evaluate how this topic usually arises. Here are a few objections to miracles:

"How can Jonah stay alive in the stomach of a fish? That's ridiculous. The digestive acid would burn him alive."

"How can you believe that the Red Sea literally parted?"

"No one can be born of a virgin."

"Dead people don't come back from the dead. There is no such thing as zombies."

A person's worldview will likely affect his view on miracles. Does the objector to miracles believe that God exists? Or does the objector believe that God does not exist? Either way, there is a method to navigating the objection.

Situation 1: *Someone believes that God exists but does not believe that miracles are possible.*

This is a fairly easy case. If God created the entire universe from literally nothing—every star, every planet, the moon, the sky, the land, the sea, every drop of water, every atom, every tree, every animal, every human, every cell, every DNA molecule—then why can't He make a dead person be alive again? That actually shouldn't be that hard for Him. If He created the entire universe out of nothing, then any other miracle is a "walk in the park."

If God created water, then He can certainly divide it like He did with the Red Sea. If God wrote the message that is DNA, then He can create human flesh from a virgin like He did with Jesus. If God can sustain space and time itself, then He can certainly sustain a person in a fish for three days like He did with Jonah.

Indeed, if Genesis 1:1 is true, then every other miracle would be "easy." Genesis 1:1 states, "In the beginning, God created the heavens and the earth." If that is true, then it is perfectly plausible that God can do any other miracle.[37]

Misconception of miracles:

People are skeptical of miracles. Most skeptics assume that miracles are synonymous with fairy tales. The word "miracle" has come to invoke images of sorcery, magic, or Santa Claus. However, the true definition of a miracle is an event that cannot be explained by natural laws. A miracle is not a parlor trick, nor is it fantasy. A miracle is simply God introducing a new event into the system which he constructed.

True, this new event does not seem to conform to natural laws. But, since God is the **author** of the framework for natural laws, He has the **author**ity to feed a new event into the system—a new event that does not adhere to specific laws that He enacted. This process is called a miracle.

Situation 2: *Someone does not believe that God exists and does not believe that miracles are possible.*

Unfortunately, the person in Situation 2 needs to start from the "Does truth exist?" argument contained in Chapter 2 of this book and proceed through subsequent chapters until arriving here.

Hopefully, after reading the evidence for God's existence as exhaustively explained in the previous chapters, this person might concede that, "Yes, God does exist." Then he can proceed to this chapter.

However, another objection will possibly arise: "Science proves miracles are impossible."

This statement is patently false. In fact, science **cannot** prove that miracles are impossible. Empirical science is the systematic observation of the natural realm in an effort to form **testable** explanations and predictions about the universe.[38] By definition, a miracle is a rare occurrence, and it cannot be repeated by scientists and therefore cannot be **tested**. If an event cannot be tested, then science cannot falsify the event. Empirical scientists interact within the framework of observable time and space (the universe), and since miracles originate outside of time and space, by definition, science is precluded from declaring miracles are impossible. Bottom line: since empirical science defines itself as conclusions drawn from **testing**, and miracles cannot be **tested**, science is not qualified to pronounce on the impossibility of miracles.

Another note about science and miracles:

Natural laws are orderly and regular. If natural laws were not regular, then how would you notice an irregularity? You wouldn't. You cannot recognize a unique event unless there is order in a system. Indeed, the very reason you can identify a "special" occurrence (miracle) is because natural laws are regular. This is so that you can point to that event as not obeying the predefined regularity. Perhaps this is a way God communicates with us. We can identify a "unique" event because God has enacted a fairly strict set of laws. This way, when one of those laws is obviously "violated," we know God has fed a new event into the system.

Your computer is governed by a relatively strict set of laws called programming. Just like the laws of nature, the laws of computer programming are orderly and regular. They are designed so that your computer behaves a certain way almost all of the time. If you accessed your computer one day and inexplicably discovered many new programs and a completely different interface, would you disbelieve and deny these new circumstances because they defy the laws of computer programming? **No!** You would rightfully infer that a person (other than you) fed new events into your computer.

In street terms, <u>someone hacked your computer</u>. The laws of computer programming were not really "violated." Someone has introduced a new event into the system.

Likewise, the universe is designed to behave a certain way almost all of the time (natural laws). By introducing new events (miracles) that appear to violate the **ordinary** laws, we can recognize God's work. Applying the computer example to a miraculous situation, the "hacker" is actually God because, yes, a miracle appears to "violate" the **ordinary** laws, but that is exactly what the event intends to accomplish. Because the event did not adhere to the ordinary laws, we can immediately recognize the event's irregularity, and it should be clear to us that the origin of this event is outside the system because the event is **extraordinary**. Someone (God) has introduced a new event into the system.

Personal Revelation:

Allow me to address an objection right now:

"If God wants to show himself to me, then why doesn't he just do a miracle now? Why doesn't he just levitate me?"

One reason is because if God levitates you, then eventually you would demand that He makes you fly. Then, after you are no longer satisfied with flying, you would demand that He send you traveling into outer space. You see the problem here? You would just keep asking for more "proof," no matter how much proof He already provides.

Plus, if God levitates you because you demand proof, then He would be forced to levitate every solicitor. If everyone was hovering upon request, then levitating would not be a rare occurrence and defeats the purpose of a miracle. The act of levitation would hold zero persuasive power. You see the problem here? No amount of "proof" would ever be sufficient.

This exchange illuminates the false line of thinking that
"If God does a miracle, then I will believe."
If He did miracles on demand, then miracles would lose their purpose (persuasive power).

We see this fact in the New Testament. In the story of the rich man and Lazarus contained in Luke 16:19–31, we learn that there are people who will not believe, even if someone rises from the dead. Miracles do not always make someone come to faith: John 12:37 says, "Though He had done so many signs before them, they still did not believe in Him."

Even if there were video of Jesus rising from the dead, some people would still claim that the film was forged, or that actors staged it. God has already given us enough evidence through his **creation** (see the "beginning of the universe," "fine-tuning," and "message" chapters), **conscience** (see the "moral law" chapter), and of course, **the person of Jesus Christ** (forthcoming "New Testament" chapters).

By demonstrating that God is the author of the universe and He has the authority to feed new events into it, we have answered that yes, miracles are possible.

In the next chapter, we will explore how to answer to the following question:

Is the New Testament true?

CHAPTER 8

IS THE NEW TESTAMENT TRUE?
(USING TEXTUAL CRITICISM)

If you were raised in Chicago like me, you have heard of the Battle of Fort Dearborn. This battle was part of the War of 1812, and it occurred on August 15, 1812, near Fort Dearborn, which was located somewhere in what is today downtown Chicago. The belligerents in this fifteen-minute skirmish were United States troops and the Potawatomi Indians.

How do you know this is true? Do you trust me? Do you trust your history teacher who told you it was true? Maybe. But if you investigated the Battle of Fort Dearborn for yourself, you would engage in the process of **historicity**.

Historicity is determining the actuality of past persons and events. This means you make a decision about these people and occurrences, a decision about whether they are facts, or whether they are myth, legend, or fiction. In short, you decide—is it true?

The reason we know the Battle of Fort Dearborn is true is because we examine the extant evidence through a test of historicity. In this and the next three chapters, we will run the New Testament through the same test as we would any other historical work. We will call it the "Historical Truth Test."

The Historical Truth Test:

1. <u>Textual Criticism</u>. Is the New Testament in the current Bible the same as the original documents? Were the original documents written promptly after the events occurred? Do we know the original documents are authentic and not forgeries?

2. <u>Principal Sources</u>. Do we have multiple, independent, and coherent accounts? Do we have eyewitness testimony? Do we have contemporary testimony? Do we have testimony from opponents of Christianity?

3. <u>Can we trust the principal sources?</u> Are the principal sources telling the truth? Are they telling thrilling but fictional stories? Or are they recording events that actually happened?

4. <u>Archeological Evidence</u>. Is there archeological evidence that comports with the New Testament?

Textual criticism. In this article, we will determine if the New Testament in the current Bible is the same as the original documents, or if the current Bible is a corrupted version, or maybe even a complete forgery.

The New Testament is twenty-seven different works by at least nine different authors collected into one volume, which we call the New Testament. The New Testament itself is then part of a larger collection of documents called The Bible.

Are there "errors" in the Bible? Has it been translated so many times that it has been corrupted? Both of these questions are alluding to a more general question:

Is the current version of the Bible **authentic**?

Yes. And we determine the authenticity of the New Testament by inspecting the early manuscripts.

Referring to the biblical era, a manuscript is a document written by hand. In the ancient world, literacy was very uncommon; therefore, having an interested party who was capable of simply writing a document was somewhat notable in itself. The writing process was time-consuming and expensive because a manuscript was likely produced on vellum, papyrus, or some other parchment. Various people copied the documents of the New Testament by hand onto a scroll or codex. They wrote these manuscripts for distribution to a wider audience. Also, they wanted to protect the original text because papyrus deteriorates fairly quickly and advanced preservation techniques had not been fully developed at the time of the copying. We can thank God that the early writers had the foresight to make these replicas.

If you know the English language, then the New Testament has been translated **once** from Greek into English (there are several different versions of the translation into English). If you are concerned about the accuracy of this **one-time** translation, then you can learn the Greek language and read the early Greek manuscripts for yourself.

There are over five thousand Greek manuscripts of New Testament text. Additionally, there are over nine thousand manuscripts in Syriac, Coptic, Latin, and Arabic. In total, there are almost **fifteen thousand** manuscripts of New Testament material.[39] To put this number in context, let's look at some other ancient works. Herodotus, known as "The Father of History" due to his contribution to the historical method, was the author of *The Histories*. There are only eight manuscripts of *The Histories*.[40] That's not a typo. Only **eight**. Yet we still call him "The Father of History." Plato made many significant contributions to philosophy and mathematics, yet we have only **250** manuscripts from his writings.[41] A contemporary of Jesus, Pliny the Elder composed an encyclopedia called *Natural History*, which served as a model for subsequent encyclopedias. There are less than **two hundred** manuscripts of this work.[42] Most people are familiar with *The Iliad* by Homer. This poem tells the story of Achilles during the Trojan War. *The Iliad* has only **643** manuscripts.[43] And the oldest manuscript of *The Iliad* is dated over <u>five hundred</u> years after it was first written! By comparison, many of the New Testament manuscripts are verified to be from within <u>fifty</u> years of the original documents!

Obviously, all of the **non**-New Testament manuscripts from antiquity combined do not even approach the wealth of manuscript support for the New Testament. Yet, no one doubts that we have a genuine copy of *The Iliad*. By the same logic, we should not doubt that we have an accurate copy of the New Testament. If we simply apply the same authenticity test we use for *The Iliad* to the New Testament, it passes with flying colors. In terms of manuscript support, the New Testament far surpasses any other accepted work from ancient times.

What makes this fact more remarkable is that in 303 AD, the Roman Emperor Diocletian ordered a mass persecution of Christians whereby the Roman Empire systematically burned hundreds, if not thousands, of additional manuscripts, but still, **fifteen thousand** survive as opposed to **643** from the next closest work (*The Iliad*). Even if Diocletian had succeeded and burned all of the manuscripts of the New Testament, you can still reconstruct almost the entire New Testament based solely on quotations from the early Church fathers (Justin Martyr, Irenaeus, Clement of Alexandria, Origen, Tertullian, et al.). Indeed, all but eleven verses from the New Testament are contained within the church fathers' collective writings, which means we have another layer of validating the original text of the New Testament.[44] By comparing the fifteen thousand manuscripts and the excerpts from the church fathers, we can be assured the original text is preserved.

You can literally see some of the New Testament manuscripts in person
at various museums and archives around the world.

Alternatively, you can visit the Center for the Study of New Testament Manuscripts (CSNTM).
You can go to their website at csntm.org
to view digital images of actual New Testament manuscripts.

The New Testament chronicles persons and events, but how early were those accounts written down?

As part of textual criticism, we critique the proximity of the time that the event occurred to when it was actually recorded. Obviously, if the source material is written closer to the affairs in question, historians consider that material to be more accurate. The events of the New Testament occur around the time of 30 AD.

It is certain that most of the New Testament was written before 100 AD (less than seventy years after the events). How do we know this? Because the early church fathers (specifically Clement, Ignatius, and Polycarp) made specific citations of twenty-five New Testament documents in their own writings before 100 AD.[45] Prior to 100 AD, these fathers composed their own letters in which they quoted an existing piece of material from the New Testament. This obviously means that the source material (the New Testament) is circulating at the time the church father is writing his own piece.

It is certain that much of the New Testament was written before 70 AD (less than forty years after the events). How do we know this? Because the temple was destroyed by the Romans in 70 AD. The temple was the cultural, economic, national, and religious center of Jerusalem. It was the most important construction of the entire region. Life in Jerusalem revolved around the temple. However, the New Testament does not record the destruction of the temple. Why is this important? The New Testament meticulously reports the cultural and religious affairs of the people of Jerusalem, but it omits the demolition of their cultural and religious center. Therefore, it must have been written prior to that destruction.

It is the year 1875 AD, and you are methodically recording the history of Chicago. Would you omit the Great Chicago Fire of 1871 AD? Of course not! You would definitely include such a momentous event in your account. In the same manner, if the New Testament authors were writing in 75 AD, then they would definitely record the crucial event of the temple ruin of 70 AD. Furthermore, Jesus predicted the destruction of the temple, so it would have been in the best interests of the writers to include that event because it would perpetuate the deity of Jesus. But the writers didn't include the destruction of temple, so it stands to reason that much of the New Testament was written before 70 AD; otherwise, they surely would have mentioned it.

It is certain that much of the New Testament was written before 62 AD (roughly thirty years after the events). How do we know this? Because James, brother of Jesus, died in 62 AD. In the New Testament book of Acts, Luke follows Paul and writes mini-biographies of the apostles, including some of their deaths. He goes so far to convince his audience of his testimony that he precisely records excruciating minutiae such as local vernacular, dialects, meteorology, topography, and obscure politicians. Yet he omits the deaths of James and Paul, two of his main subjects. Paul died during the reign of Emperor Nero, which ended in 68 AD. James died in 62 AD at the hands of the Sanhedrin (an incident reported by the non-Christian writer Josephus). Why would Luke go through painstaking lengths to document the details of the apostles but not talk about the deaths of Paul and James? The answer is simple: because he wrote them before their demise. Luke records the deaths of Stephen and James, the brother of John, so we know he writes on the subject of martyrdom. But the glaring omission of the deaths of Paul and James speaks volumes—that Luke's works were written prior to 62 AD.[46] Furthermore, Paul's own letters, which comprise an ample amount of the New Testament, obviously had to have been written prior to his death, which occurred before 68 AD.

It is certain that many of the New Testament elements were in circulation before 40 AD (less than **ten** years after the events). How do we know this? First Corinthians 15:3–7 states, "*For I delivered to you as of first importance **what I also received**: that Christ died for our sins in accordance with the Scriptures, that he was buried, that he was raised on the third day in accordance with the Scriptures, and that he appeared to Cephas, then to the twelve. Then he appeared to more than five hundred brothers at one time, most of whom are still alive, though some have fallen asleep. Then he appeared to James, then to all the apostles.*"

This passage from the New Testament is a type of "creed." It was an oral recitation of early Christians. When I say "early" Christians in this case, I am referring to people who were alive at the time of Jesus' death and resurrection, and who perhaps witnessed it. Most of these early Christians were illiterate, so in order to relay their testimony, they constructed rhythmic sayings and possibly even hymns so that they could easily remember and recall what actually occurred. This is how the gospel was spread immediately after the events. As you can see in 1 Corinthians 15:3–7, Paul is telling us that he heard this "creed" from someone else ("what I also received"). First Corinthians is dated to be one of the first completed works of the New Testament (roughly 40 AD).[47] Therefore, if he included this oral creed in his epistle, then it was in circulation prior to his writing it.

An interesting note about this "creed" is that Paul is essentially inviting people to investigate the resurrection for themselves. He is inciting them by basically saying, "If you don't believe me, ask all these other people who witnessed the resurrection in the flesh." He knows it is true, so he can issue such a challenge. Likewise, there are other "creeds" that are cited in the New Testament, which demonstrates that the fundamentals of the gospel were being attested to within a short time after the resurrection. Furthermore, Paul's letters serve as instructions to **existing** churches. Clearly, these Christian churches were established at the time of Paul's epistles. How else could he be giving them directions? For this reason, we can conclude elements of the New Testament were circulating prior to his letters.

Based on the evidence presented in this chapter, the New Testament contains an embarrassment of riches in relation to positive textual criticism. The New Testament has completely exceeded step one in what we will call the "Historical Truth Test." Demonstrating the authenticity of the New Testament by using this evidence is the first step toward answering the question: Is the New Testament true?

In the next chapter, we will explore the principal sources of the New Testament in an effort to answer the following question:

Is the New Testament true?

IS THE NEW TESTAMENT TRUE?
(USING THE PRINCIPAL SOURCES)

Do you believe that the Battle of Fort Dearborn actually occurred? We briefly touched on this topic in the previous chapter. The reason we know the Battle of Fort Dearborn is true is because we can examine the extant evidence through a test of historicity. To progress in this endeavor, let's inspect the principal sources of the Battle of Fort Dearborn.

There are four principal sources of this incident. One source is the journal of Nathan Heald, the commander of the United States troops in the battle.[48] Heald Square Monument, located on Wacker Drive and Wabash Avenue in Chicago, was erected in his honor. Another source is Corporal Walter K. Jordan, who briefly describes the skirmish in a letter to his wife.[49] The third principal source is a narrative from United States Lieutenant Linai Thomas Helm.[50] The final principal source of the battle is an oral recollection from John Kinzie, a fur trader.[51] Even though Kinzie was technically a British citizen, he was known to have aided the Americans. Kinzie Avenue (400 North) in Chicago is named after him. He allegedly witnessed the battle and a writer later recorded his version of events. Kinzie killed an interpreter who worked at Fort Dearborn. This man's job was to translate Native American languages into English for the Americans and the British. Kinzie was later exonerated of the crime via a self-defense claim. This case is known as "Chicago's First Murder."

Now, there are four principal sources from the Battle of Fort Dearborn, and all claim to be eyewitnesses. All of these accounts are from the pro-American side of the war. There are no primary sources written by opponents of America, yet there is no doubt that this conflict actually occurred. So, in terms of principal sources, how does the New Testament compare?

Remember, we will run the New Testament through the same test as we would any other historical work: the Historical Truth Test.

The Historical Truth Test:

1. <u>Textual Criticism</u>. Is the New Testament in the current Bible the same as the original documents? Were the original documents written promptly after the events occurred? Do we know the original documents are authentic and not forgeries? **Covered in Chapter 8**.

2. <u>Principal Sources</u>. Do we have multiple, independent, and coherent accounts? Do we have eyewitness testimony? Do we have contemporary testimony? Do we have testimony from opponents of Christianity?

3. <u>Can we trust the principal sources</u>? Are the principal sources telling the truth? Are they telling thrilling, but fictional stories? Or, are they recording events that actually happened?

4. <u>Archeological Evidence</u>. Is there archeological evidence that comports with the New Testament?

Principal Sources. In this chapter, we will examine the New Testament principal sources.

Eyewitnesses. Historians consider eyewitness testimony to be the "best" type of historical evidence. Obviously, if events have an abundance of eyewitness testimony, then the accounts are considered accurate.

How much eyewitness testimony do we have in the New Testament?

Some of the authors of the twenty-seven books are eyewitness.

Matthew the apostle, also known as "Levi," was a disciple of Jesus. Therefore, he literally saw the events he is describing in the *Gospel According to Matthew*, which is the first book of the New Testament. John the apostle, known as the one "whom Jesus loved," was also a disciple of Jesus. He saw Jesus crucified with his own two eyes. He is the author of five books of the New Testament: the *Gospel According to John*, *1 John*, *2 John*, *3 John*, and *Revelation*. Peter, also known as "Cephas," is the rock upon which Jesus built his church, and a disciple of Christ. He wrote two books of the New Testament. Peter's epistles are eyewitness accounts because he was intimately involved in the events he describes. The New Testament book of James was a letter written by James "the Just," sometimes referred to as "the brother of Jesus" due to him being either a relative or close family friend of Jesus. As we learned in the previous chapter, he was martyred in 62 AD. Obviously, being a kinsman of Jesus, James had unique inside perspective to the events of the New Testament. This also applies to the New Testament book of Jude who is called the brother of James the Just. Jude is the author of the *Epistle of Jude*, which is the penultimate work of the New Testament. Based on authorship alone, at least five of the writers of the New Testament were eyewitnesses. These authors completed ten of the twenty-seven books of the New Testament.

And there's more.

Even though it is debated that Luke the evangelist was himself an eyewitness, he specifically claims that the *Gospel According to Luke* and the *Acts of the Apostles* (two New Testament books) are legitimate eyewitness accounts.

<u>Luke 1:1–4</u>. *"Inasmuch as many have undertaken to compile a narrative of the things that have been accomplished among us, just as those who from the beginning were **eyewitnesses** and ministers of the word have delivered them to us, it seemed good to me also, having followed all things closely for some time past, to **write an orderly account** for you, most excellent Theophilus, that you may have certainty concerning the things you have been taught."*

<u>Acts 1:1–3</u>. *"In the **first book**, O Theophilus, I have dealt with all that Jesus began to do and teach, until the day when he was taken up, after he had given commands through the Holy Spirit to the apostles whom he had chosen. He presented himself alive to them after his suffering **by many proofs**, appearing to them during forty days and speaking about the kingdom of God."*

In Acts 1, we see that Luke is writing to a Roman official named "Theophilus." He refers to his gospel ("first book"), which he specifically says was compiled from eyewitness testimony. Throughout his works, Luke painstakingly identifies eyewitnesses as his primary sources. Here are just a few instances of Luke invoking firsthand accounts: Acts 1:23, Acts 2:32, Acts 3:15, Acts 4:1–20, Acts 5:30–32, Acts 10:39–40.

Luke was as an investigative reporter. His goal was to locate as many witnesses as possible, interview them, and record their versions of events into a coherent account for Theophilus. He is so concerned with the authenticity of his work that he meticulously documents excruciating minutiae such as local slang, geography, weather patterns, currency, weights and measures, as well as obscure politicians and bureaucrats. Luke values eyewitnesses over all other forms of testimony. Similarly, if not as exhaustively, the author of *Hebrews* claims to have interviewed eyewitnesses as well (Hebrews 2:3–4).

Another author of the New Testament may have been an eyewitness. The *Gospel According to Mark* was written by Mark the evangelist, who was a companion and translator for Peter during his missions. As we have noted, Peter was an eyewitness of the events of the New Testament; therefore, Mark was leveraging Peter's eyewitness testimony in his own account. Additionally, Mark himself was likely an eyewitness because he is considered one of the first seventy disciples.

The principal sources of the New Testament include an abundance of eyewitness testimony. Nothing from the ancient world is in the same universe in regard to having records from people who literally saw the events.

There is another layer of verification of the principal sources.

Contemporary sources. Like eyewitness testimony, contemporary sources are people who were alive at the time of the events they are describing.

One of these contemporary sources is Paul. Sometimes called "Saul," Paul was a Roman citizen and Jewish Pharisee who ruthlessly persecuted Christians until he converted at some point in the 30s AD. Paul wrote or co-wrote at least thirteen books of the New Testament. He was a contemporary of Jesus. He had virtually unlimited access to people who were eyewitnesses and used them extensively in his letters. He often cites "creeds," which he received from eyewitnesses. Because he was a contemporary of the New Testament occurrences, Paul is in a position to challenge his audience to investigate his claims for themselves. For example, he tells Governor Festus that the events of the crucifixion and resurrection did not "happen in a corner" (Acts 26).

That is, if Festus is skeptical of Paul's claims, Festus could interview and ask eyewitnesses and make a decision for himself. He issues the same challenge in 1 Corinthians 15. He provides a list of people who witnessed the resurrection so that his readers can test the veracity of his account (this exchange is covered in detail in Chapter 8).

Timothy is another contemporary source of the New Testament. He is named in the text as the co-author of *2 Corinthians, Philippians, Colossians, 1 Thessalonians, 2 Thessalonians,* and *Philemon*. Another contemporary source of the New Testament is Silas, who is mentioned as the co-author of *1 and 2 Thessalonians* and *1 Peter*. Sosthenes is another contemporary source, as he is listed as the co-author of *1 Corinthians*.

The New Testament is overflowing with eyewitness and contemporary sources. Most of these sources are people who were Christian. Do we have any testimony from opponents of Christianity?

Non-Christian Sources. Josephus, Tacitus, Pliny the Younger, Phlegon, Thallus, Suetonius, Lucian, Celsus, Mara Bar-Serapion, and the Jewish *Talmud* are all **non**-Christian sources that mention Jesus. All **ten** of these sources are dated within 150 years of Jesus. Tiberius Caesar was the Roman Emperor during most of Jesus' life. How many non-Christian sources mention Tiberius within 150 years? **Nine**. That's right—only **nine**.

The most "powerful" person alive at the time of Jesus was mentioned **less** often than our Lord. And that number only includes **non**-Christian sources. If you include all sources from within 150 years, Jesus is identified by **forty-three** separate sources whereas Tiberius is listed by ten.[52] Yet no one doubts Tiberius Caesar existed. If we apply the same test to Jesus, he is more believable than anyone from that time period.

All I have to say is, look at the scoreboard: **43** to **10**.

The New Testament is unquestionably replete with positive principal source material. The New Testament has completely exceeded Steps 1 and 2 in the Historical Truth Test. Presenting the principal sources of the New Testament is another step toward answering the question: Is the New Testament true?

However, were these sources telling the truth? Can we trust them? Did they record events that actually occurred or were they telling fictitious stories?

In the next chapter, we will explore the trustworthiness of the New Testament in an effort to answer the following question:

Is the New Testament true?

CHAPTER 10

IS THE NEW TESTAMENT TRUE?
(USING THE TRUSTWORTHINESS OF THE PRINCIPLE SOURCES)

Do you believe that the Battle of Fort Dearborn actually occurred? In the previous two chapters, we have been using this topic as the backdrop for our Historical Truth Test. We have seen that there are four principal sources from the Battle of Fort Dearborn. These sources all claim to be eyewitnesses.

However...

All of these accounts are from the pro-American side of the war. There are no primary sources written by opponents of America. Does this mean that the sources are not trustworthy since they were biased for America? Also, one of the sources was John Kinzie, who was a self-admitted killer (he was exonerated of murder by a self-defense claim). How can we trust him if he killed somebody?

Even further, the Americans at the fort were desperate for help. How do we know that the primary sources didn't invent or embellish their accounts to receive funding and aid from the federal government? A skeptic can claim that they concocted the story for money, power, and fame.

Despite these objections, no legitimate historian has any doubt that the Battle of Fort Dearborn actually occurred. The central points of their accounts are: the Americans lost the battle, sixty-seven people died, others were captured, and the fort was burned to the ground. These points are indisputable despite the objections raised in the previous paragraphs. We believe these events actually happened.

In the same vein, the central points of the New Testament (truly the entire Bible) are the crucifixion and resurrection of Jesus. Are the principal sources of these events trustworthy, and are they recording events that actually occurred?

Remember, we will run the New Testament through the same test as we would any other historical work, the Historical Truth Test.

The Historical Truth Test:

1. <u>Textual Criticism</u>. Is the New Testament in the current Bible the same as the original documents? Were the original documents written promptly after the events occurred? Do we know the original documents are authentic and not forgeries? **Covered in Chapter 8.**

2. <u>Principal Sources</u>. Do we have multiple, independent, and coherent accounts? Do we have eyewitness testimony? Do we have contemporary testimony? Do we have testimony from opponents of Christianity? **Covered in Chapter 9.**

3. <u>Can we trust the principal sources?</u> Are the principal sources telling the truth? Are they telling thrilling but fictional stories? Or are they recording events that actually happened?

4. <u>Archeological Evidence</u>. Is there archeological evidence that comports with the New Testament?

Can we trust the principal sources? In this chapter, we will examine the trustworthiness and actuality of the accounts of the crucifixion and resurrection.

Martyrdom. Other than being Christian, what do Matthew, Mark, Luke, Peter, James the Just, James the Son of Zebedee, Bartholomew, Andrew, Thomas, Jude, Matthias, Barnabas, Stephen, Phillip, and Paul have in common? They were all murdered because they were Christian. They all claimed that Jesus rose from the dead, and they were killed for it. Matthew was gored with a sword in Ethiopia. Mark was dragged by a horse through the streets of Egypt until he was dead. Luke was hanged. Peter was crucified (possibly upside-down). James the Just was defenestrated from the temple in Jerusalem. James, son of Zebedee, was beheaded. Bartholomew was flogged to death or crucified. Andrew was crucified (possibly on an X-shaped cross). Thomas was impaled with a spear in India. Jude was killed by a barrage of arrows like a modern-day firing squad. Matthias was stoned to death. Barnabas was stoned to death. Stephen was stoned to death. Phillip was crucified. Paul was beheaded. John, the only apostle who died peacefully, was boiled alive in Rome. After the giant basin of seething hot oil did not kill him, the authorities banished him to the island of Patmos, where he lived under exile. All of the aforementioned martyrs received beatings and treacherous torture preceding their deaths.[53] How does the martyrdom of the apostles demonstrate that they were telling the truth in the New Testament?

If you **knew** something was a lie, would you die for it? There have been tales of people dying for lies that they **believed** to be true, but people do not willingly die for a lie they **know** to be false. In other words, the apostles were in a position to **know** if Jesus rose from the dead. We clearly established this point in the previous chapter. Many of them were eyewitnesses and all were contemporaries. They **knew** the truth of whether or not Jesus rose from the dead. If Jesus did not rise from the dead, why would they die for that, **knowing** it was false? They could have easily said, "Jesus did not rise from the dead" and escaped death, or at least hasten the torture leading up to it. But they all willingly died for Him, claiming, "Jesus rose from the dead."

Someone might claim, "The apostles just made it up for money, power, or fame!"

What did the apostles have to gain by inventing Christianity? Money? Power? Fame? No. All of them were persecuted, were scourged, and were heinously murdered in the most painful manners imaginable (save for John). All of them died in destitution and suffering. No one would bear these afflictions for something they **know** is a lie. They had zero motivation to make it up. Their reward was a vicious beating and death. This gives us good reason to believe that the New Testament writers knew Jesus truly rose from the dead and that the resurrection actually occurred.[54]

Radical Change in Beliefs and Behavior. Before these apostles died, they abandoned or minimized millenniums-old religious and cultural traditions. Most of the apostles were Jewish. The Jews required the following beliefs and behavior: animal sacrifice, circumcision, ritual Laws of Moses, single-person monotheism, stringent observance of the Sabbath, and they believed in a messiah of worldly conquest. These beliefs and behaviors had been embedded in Jewish culture and theology for at least 1,500 years prior to the time of the apostles. To not behave in alignment with these beliefs was to risk severe punishment and even death. Yet the apostles, most of whom were strictly bound to these ideas, abandoned or minimized them in an instant. Not only did they claim these behaviors were no longer necessary due to their fulfillment in Christ, they observed new practices such as baptism and communion. Why would these apostles risk their lives by claiming deeply ingrained traditions were unneeded due to the life and resurrection of Jesus? Because the apostles knew that the resurrection actually occurred. And they were in a position to know if it happened. This gives us another reason to believe they were providing true accounts in the New Testament.[55]

Unflattering Details. If you were fabricating a story about one of your experiences, would you include embarrassing details about yourself and the protagonist of the story? Or, since you were making it up anyway, would you make yourself look better? The honest answer is that most of us would insert good stuff and omit bad stuff. If we are going to make something up, we might as well make ourselves look good in the process.

Conversely, throughout the New Testament, the writers include unflattering details about themselves. They are portrayed as cowards—they forsake Jesus during his trial, torture, and death. They are portrayed as doubters and deniers: Thomas doubts the resurrection even though he sees Jesus with his own two eyes, and Peter denies Jesus three times. They are portrayed as being daft; they repeatedly misunderstand or express a complete failure to comprehend what Jesus is telling them. They are apathetic. They fall asleep on Jesus in his hour of need. Mark, a companion of Peter, writes that Jesus calls Peter, "Satan." If Mark were making up the story, why would he have Jesus refer to his own friend as "Satan" (and Peter is supposed to be the "rock" of the church!)? Almost surely, the primary sources would have omitted these unflattering details if they were making up the story.

Furthermore, the writers include statements from others about Jesus that could be embarrassing to Him. He is considered, "out of his mind," "a drunkard," and "a madman." Jesus' own family doesn't believe Him. In one episode, He allows a prostitute to wipe his feet. These things, if not properly understood, could be very incriminating to someone who claims to be God (Jesus). But since the writers included these unflattering details, it gives us another reason to believe they were not lying about their accounts in the New Testament.

Women Were the First Witnesses. In the time period of the resurrection, a woman's testimony was completely debased. In fact, a woman was forbidden to testify during trials because she was not regarded as a credible witness. Despite this fact, the New Testament reports that women were the first witnesses to the resurrection. If the primary sources were inventing the story, they would **not** have made women the first witnesses because female accounts were not acceptable. If they were falsifying an account, then they would insert the most prestigious witnesses (men). But they didn't. They stuck to the truth. The fact that the primary sources record women as the first witnesses to the resurrection gives us another reason to believe that the writers were being truthful and not simply inventing a story.[56]

Non-Christian Sources. As we discussed, the Battle of Fort Dearborn has zero "non-American" sources. Someone could say that the Battle of Fort Dearborn is false because the accounts are biased. Likewise, someone might claim that the resurrection is false because the accounts are biased.

Firstly, just because an account is biased, does that mean that it is false? **NO**. For example, if you are robbed at gunpoint, when the police investigate the crime, do they discard your account because you are biased? **NO**. Even though you might be "biased" against the robber because he stole from you, your testimony is accepted as "true" because you were an eyewitness, just like many of the New Testament writers.

Furthermore, regarding the claim that the New Testament is written by biased sources, let's leave the Bible out of it. Using **non-Christian** sources alone, what can we learn about Jesus? (As we saw in the previous chapter, there are ten **non**-Christian sources about Jesus within 150 years of His life while there are only nine about Tiberius Caesar, who was the Roman emperor during much of Jesus' life.)

This is what we know about Jesus from those ten non-Christian sources:

Jesus was a virtuous man who lived during the age of Tiberius Caesar. Jesus performed works of wonder. One of his kin was named James. People claimed He was the Messiah, fulfilling the prophecy of the Old Testament. He was crucified under the auspices of Pontius Pilate. His crucifixion occurred near Passover. His crucifixion was accompanied by an earthquake and unusual darkness. He was buried in a tomb protected by guards. His followers were convinced He rose from the dead. His followers were willing to die for claiming that the resurrection was true. Christianity swiftly and explosively spread throughout the Mediterranean, including the city of Rome. His followers, called "Christians," refused to bow to the Roman gods and instead worshipped Jesus as God, a practice for which they were killed.[57]

Does this sound familiar? **Yes!** This **non-Christian** account of Jesus' life is congruent with the New Testament! Let's focus on the crucifixion and resurrection, the central tenets of Christianity:

The **non**-Christian sources record that Jesus was crucified and that He was buried in a tomb protected by a number of guards. Now, if the non-Christian authorities wanted to disprove the resurrection, all they had to do was simply produce the dead body of Jesus. This would mean He did not rise from the dead. This would mean that Christianity is false.

So, did they produce the dead body?

NO. Even though they admit he was crucified and buried, <u>THEY COULD NOT PRODUCE THE DEAD BODY OF JESUS.</u>

What's their explanation?

Jesus' disciples stole the body while the guards were asleep.

This claim is illogical and unreasonable for a number of reasons.

First, the guards were highly trained. They deployed measures to prevent precisely the possibility of falling asleep (personnel rotation, check-ins, walking perimeter). Furthermore, falling asleep on duty was a harsh offense. The guards would suffer severe punishment for falling asleep, and they had additional motivation to successfully guard the tomb of Jesus given the scandalous publicity of his case.

Secondly, the tomb was encased by an enormous rock. To prevent tomb robbers (some people were buried with jewels and heirlooms), sometimes an apparatus had to be utilized to remove the giant stone. The disciples did not have the means or strength to "unlock" the tomb. Even if the disciples acquired the equipment to move the rock, the removal process would have been very noisy and the "sleeping guards" would have awoke from the ruckus.

Thirdly, if the guards were asleep, how could they know that "the disciples stole the body"? How could the guards make ANY claim as to what happened if they were asleep? A person can't observe something if he is sleeping. Based on this obvious fact alone, the "sleeping guards excuse" is utterly absurd.

This evidence demonstrates that the New Testament consists of trustworthy primary source material that reports events that actually happened. Additionally, non-Christian sources external of, and hostile to, Christianity verify the fundamental episodes of the New Testament. The New Testament has completely exceeded Steps 1, 2, and 3 in the Historical Truth Test. Presenting the trustworthiness of the principal sources is another step toward answering the question: is the New Testament true?

And still, we have another method of confirming the answer to that question: archeology.

In the next chapter, we will explore the archeological evidence that comports with the New Testament in an effort to answer the following question:

Is the New Testament True?

Even if the Bible did not exist,
what could you learn from the other historical sources external of the Bible?

Going from the upper left quadrant to the right, Jesus was a virtuous man who worked
wonders. Jesus was crucified, a death that was accompanied by an earthquake and darkness.
Many people claimed to have seen him risen from the dead, and they were in a positon to
know if that claim was true or false. Many of these people were killed for proclaiming that
assertion was true and refusing to say it was false.

CHAPTER 11

IS THE NEW TESTAMENT TRUE?
(USING ARCHEOLOGY)

Do you believe that the Battle of Fort Dearborn actually occurred? In the previous three chapters, we have been using this topic as the backdrop for our Historical Truth Test. We discussed the principal sources of the Battle of Fort Dearborn to determine if the conflict actually happened. Another layer of verification is to examine the archeological evidence. While archeology alone cannot prove the truth of an account, it can help corroborate the events in question.

Do we have any archeological evidence supporting the accounts of the Battle of Fort Dearborn?

Not really. After the battle, the anti-American forces burned the fort to the ground. Nothing was left. If you recall from the previous chapters, one of the principal sources of the battle was John Kinzie. His daughter, Juliette Kinzie, who was five years old at the time of the battle, reported that the skirmish started at a large tree near what is today 18th Street and Prairie Avenue.[58] She made this claim shortly before 1870 (more than fifty years after the event). On May 16, 1894 (more than eighty years after the event), the tree at issue was blown over during a storm. Luckily, a section of the trunk was preserved at the Chicago Historical Society. The diameter of the trunk is measured to be about three feet. Based on a botanical study, the tree could not be more than eighty years old in 1894.[59] What does this mean? The tree was **not** growing at the time of the Battle in 1812. Therefore, there isn't any verifiable archeological evidence supporting the accounts of the Battle of Fort Dearborn. Despite this fact, no legitimate historian has any doubt that this conflict actually occurred.

Since we believe that this event occurred absent of archeological evidence, certainly we should believe events that **do** have the support of archeological evidence.

Do we have any archeological evidence supporting the accounts of the New Testament?

Remember, we will run the New Testament through the same test as we would any other work, the Historical Truth Test.

The Historical Truth Test:

1. <u>Textual Criticism</u>. Is the New Testament in the current Bible the same as the original documents? Were the original documents written promptly after the events occurred? Do we know the original documents are authentic and not forgeries? **Covered in Chapter 8.**

2. <u>Principal Sources</u>. Do we have multiple, independent, and coherent accounts? Do we have eyewitness testimony? Do we have contemporary testimony? Do we have testimony from opponents of Christianity? **Covered in Chapter 9.**

3. <u>Can we trust the principal sources?</u> Are the principal sources telling the truth? Are they telling thrilling but fictional stories? Or, are they recording events that actually happened? **Covered in Chapter 10.**

4. <u>Archeological Evidence</u>. Is there archeological evidence that comports with the New Testament?

Archeological Evidence. In this chapter, we will examine the archeological evidence that supports the New Testament. Again, archeological evidence alone does not completely prove an event occurred, but we can support the truth of the New Testament by providing evidence from archeology that comports with the New Testament accounts.

House of Peter. The ancient fishing village of Capernaum was the hometown of Peter, Andrew, James the Son of Zebedee, and John. Ever since 1838, when the ruins of Capernaum were discovered, excavations of the site have been ongoing.[60] During one of the digs, the archeologists found a complex array of private dwellings built in the first century AD (the time of Jesus). The roofs were constructed with wood beams covered in thatch emulsified in mud. This archeological discovery supports the story of Jesus forgiving and healing the paralytic man who was lowered down through the ceiling (Mark 2:1–12). Furthermore, one of these houses is identified as the house of Peter due to various mosaics painted on the walls.

Crucified Corpse. In 1968 the corpse of a man was unearthed in Jerusalem. This man, identified as Jehohanan the son of Hagkol, was executed by crucifixion in the first century AD (the time of Jesus). This finding is important because it corroborates the New Testament claim that the Romans used crucifixion as a form of capital punishment. Upon examination of the corpse of Jehohanan, archeologists have concluded his arms were stretched out and nailed (his feet were also nailed) to a two-beamed Latin cross, which is congruent with how the New Testament depicts the crucifixion of Jesus.

Pilate Stone. Speaking of the crucifixion of Jesus, the New Testament reports that Pontius Pilate had the earthly authority to order it. In 1961 a block of carved limestone was discovered in Caesarea, Israel. This stone contains an inscription that mentions "Pontius Pilatus" as a "Prefect."[61] This supports the New Testament accounts of Pontius Pilate.

Archeologists have uncovered a house supporting the account of Jesus healing a paralytic man, discussed in the New Testament documents written by Matthew, Mark, and Luke.

Caiaphas Ossuary. The high priest who delivered Jesus to Pilate was Caiaphas. We have his ossuary. An ossuary is a bone box, similar to a coffin. In the second temple period, the customary Jewish burial process was to lay a body in a "cave" (tomb) and adorn it with alms and oils. After some time, the family would transfer the bones into an ossuary due to the fact they believed in a bodily resurrection of the dead. In 1990 one such ossuary was discovered. This ossuary contained the engraving, "Joseph, son of Caiaphas." Scholars have identified this as the skeletal remains of Caiaphas, the high priest who delivered Jesus up to be crucified.[62]

James Ossuary. In 2002 another important ossuary was discovered. This box contained the epigraph, "James son of Joseph, brother of Jesus." In previous chapters, we discussed that James was a kinsman or close family friend ("brother") of Jesus. James wrote the *Epistle of James* in the New Testament. An analysis of the carving, performed in March 2014 by a team of three notable archeologists, confirms the authenticity of the ossuary and inscription.[63] Obviously, this is a significant finding due to the fact it provides archeological evidence of the existence of Jesus Christ.

Provided the overwhelming positive evidence amassed in Chapters 8 through 11, we have demonstrated the affirmative answer to the following question:

Is the New Testament true?

YES.

Despite the truth of the New Testament as readily apparent in Chapters 8 through 11, there still may be objections:

Okay. The New Testament seems to be true, but why are there **contradictions** in it?

There are no contradictions in the New Testament. Before we directly verify the absence of contradictions in the New Testament, do apparent contradictions in eyewitness testimony mean the events in question never happened?

To answer this question, let's go back and look at the Battle of Fort Dearborn. Among the principal sources writing about the conflict, there are several discrepancies. For example, the witnesses differ in the number of combatants. Also, Nathan Heald and John Kinzie tell us that the skirmish took place at completely different locations! Should we pretend the entire battle didn't happen due to these apparent contradictions? **No**! These are not really "contradictions"; these are **divergent details**. The reason that the number of combatants are disparate between the reports is because the witnesses didn't stop in the middle of the battle and take a precise headcount. Plus, their specific encounters with the enemy may have been different. Heald and Kinzie may have recorded the location differently due to the fact there weren't as many distinctive landmarks such as street signs, tall buildings, etc. Despite the apparent contradictions, we still know the Battle of Fort Dearborn actually occurred.

Again, there are no contradictions in the New Testament. There are **divergent details**. For example, the *Gospel According to Matthew* says there was an angel at the vacant tomb of Jesus. The *Gospel According to John* reports that there were two angels. Isn't that a contradiction? **No**! Matthew does not say that there was **only** one angel. He simply provides a detail about there being **an** angel of particular prominence. This is not a contradiction. It is a divergent detail.

Another apparent contradiction is the Sermon on the Mount. Matthew records it as taking place on a mount. Luke records it taking place on a "level place." Isn't that a contradiction? **No**! It is certainly possible that Jesus preached the same sermon more than once, so Matthew and Luke were recording the same repeated oratory. Another explanation is that the mount in question had a plateau so Jesus went up the mount but settled on a "level place" to speak. This is clearly not a contradiction.

Interestingly, divergent details actually point to the authenticity of historical accounts. Why? Because it shows that the writers were not conspiring to devise a fictitious story. If the writers were inventing a story together, they would have collaborated to make sure they ironed out every detail to be the exact same. Since the New Testament contains divergent, but not contradictory, details, we have reason to believe that the witnesses were authentic, and not in collusion.

Okay. The New Testament seems to be true, but **what about the Old Testament?**

We can handle this objection by running the Old Testament through our Historical Truth Test. However, that exhausting task is unnecessary because we have a trump card: **Jesus**. We have demonstrated that the New Testament is true. After that process, the truth of the Old Testament is fairly simple: the New Testament tells us that the Old Testament is true.

I don't have the space to provide every example, but the New Testament is filled with confirmations of the Old Testament. Jesus himself uses terms like, "It is written" or, "Haven't you read" when referring to Old Testament Scripture (Matthew 19:4, Mark 12:26, Matthew 22:31, Luke 18:20). This means that Jesus is using the Old Testament truths to prove his points. Furthermore, Jesus tells us that the Old Testament Scriptures testify to or are being fulfilled in Him (Matthew 5:17, John 5:39–47, Luke 24:25–27, Matthew 26:53–56). Jesus would only say these things if the Old Testament is true. The New Testament is replete with affirmations of the Old Testament. Therefore, once we have demonstrated the truth of the New Testament, the Old Testament must also be true.

At this point through the first eleven chapters, we have provided a positive presentation for the truth of Christianity. Unfortunately, it is unlikely that we have ample time to make this comprehensive case that Christianity is true. Oftentimes, we are required to respond to objections.

In the next chapter, we will explore how to handle the objection:

"What about evolution?"

CHAPTER 12

WHAT ABOUT EVOLUTION?

Now that we have presented a positive case for Christianity by using the previous eleven chapters, we will need to know how to effectively navigate common objections to Christianity. Oftentimes, our opportunity to defend Christianity arises from an objection. That is, rather than having the chance to present a positive case using the framework provided in this book, we are obliged to respond to someone who regurgitates a fictitious slogan. This person is issuing an objection to Christianity. From my experience, this person probably has not examined his own objection. He might be repeating a sound bite. In the next several chapters, I will write about how to respond to common objections.

The first step to responding to an objection is to **ask a question**. The question should compel the objector to elaborate on his contention. You will find that the person usually doesn't have any evidence. He will simply repeat or rephrase his original catchphrase.

For example, someone might say, "Evolution is true," or "Evolution proves Christianity is false."

How do you respond?

You should ask, "**What do you mean by evolution?**"

This question will illuminate the fact that the objector doesn't rightly understand his own position.

Once he responds with his refrain, you should **ask another question**.

Do you mean <u>micro-evolution</u> or <u>macro-evolution?</u>

<u>**Micro-evolution**</u> is observable variance in physical or behavioral traits within the population of a species. Then, one of these traits is selected as advantageous for reproduction or survival. The result is that the trait is passed down to offspring who then also reproduce and pass the trait down again. This process continues until the population of the species exhibits the advantageous trait in larger numbers.

The most common example is "Darwin's Finches." Charles Darwin, the propagator of the theory of evolution, observed that a certain group of finches possessed large, powerful beaks while another group had smaller beaks. Through his study, he concluded that the stronger beaks were more advantageous for the survival of the finches because the stronger beaks were more capable of cracking tougher seeds. Since these finches could eat more seeds, they had a better chance of survival; therefore, they were in a position to reproduce in greater numbers. The result is that a larger portion of the entire finch population contained these larger-beaked birds.[64]

This is an example of **micro-evolution**. Overall, this theory is likely true. Given the data, adaptation **within** a species seems to be observable through empirical evidence. Think about dogs: the largest dog in the world is a Great Dane. The smallest dog is an Affenpinscher. Through the process of selecting certain traits (big body or small body) within the dog population, breeders can deliver a dog as big as a Great Dane or as small as an Affenpinscher. However, both the Great Dane and the Affenpinscher are **DOGS**. No matter which traits are continuously selected, the breeders are confined to genetic limits; they cannot break the **DOG** species. This brings us to macro-evolution.

Macro-evolution is where an entirely new **kind** of creature comes into existence through a blind, unguided process of micro-evolution. The basic thesis of macro-evolution is that every single living thing has descended from a common ancestor. From this common ancestor, through the process of micro-evolution, new **kinds** of creatures are formed. Macro-evolution contends that every bacteria, every algae, every plant, every tree, every insect, every animal, every human came into being from the same exact organism. Likely, in the evolutionist's view, this organism was a self-replicating single cell. Then, through a process of gradual changes within the population of the organism, new **kinds** of creatures were formed through micro-evolution (selection on advantageous traits).

Do we have any evidence for <u>macro-evolution</u>?

NO. The dog breeding example from above seems to contradict macro-evolution. No matter what dog breeders do, they cannot create anything other than a **DOG**. The evolutionist will argue that dog breeding has not been performed long enough for new **kinds** to evolve from dogs. They say, "Give it more time." This contention is pure speculation, so it's a bad argument. However, it's a bad argument for a much better reason. We **have** given it more time through long-term evolutionary experiments. What is the result? Let's look:

Fruit Fly Experiments

In 1980 a group of scientists purposely selected genes in a population of fruit flies for reproduction. Since a fruit fly has a very short generational life span, scientists are able to manipulate genes to imitate thousands of years of the micro-evolutionary process in an effort to create a new **kind** of organism. What was the result of their experiments? Mutant fruit flies. Some of the resultant fruit flies have wings growing out of their heads. Others don't have any wings. But they are all still **fruit flies**. Building on the 1980 experiment, another group of researchers started their own study in 1991. Once again, the scientists tried to aid the micro-evolutionary process by selecting advantageous gene traits within the population in an effort to bring new **kinds** into being. The result? More **fruit flies**. These experiments have been so intense and long-term that they have performed what is the equivalent to 12,000 years of human evolution! But they have not been able to break genetic limits. They still have **fruit flies**.[65]

Objection! Give it more time!

Okay. Let's do that:

E. Coli Bacteria Experiments

Similar to the fruit fly experiments, scientists at Michigan State University have been studying evolution in bacteria for over twenty-five years (since 1988). E. coli bacteria was chosen for this research due to the fact that the generational life span of E. coli is twenty to thirty minutes. They have performed studies on 60,000 generations of bacteria, which is the equivalent to 2.4 million years of human evolution! After this painstaking evolutionary process of trying to bring a new **kind** into existence from E. coli, what do these scientists have?

E. coli bacteria. That's right; no matter how hard they try, they cannot break genetic limits. They still have **E. coli bacteria** after 60,000 generations of evolution.[66] After what is equivalent to 2.4 million years of human evolution, the scientists have provided evidence that **macro-evolution is false**.

Furthermore, notice that micro-evolution in nature is a blind, unguided process. Conversely, the micro-evolutionary process imitated in a laboratory is aided by intelligent minds—the minds of the scientists. They are purposely **trying** to create a new **kind** by intelligently selecting the advantageous genes for reproduction. But they still cannot incite macro-evolution! If all of their experiments prove that macro-evolution cannot occur **with** intelligent intervention, how can we believe that macro-evolution can occur **without** an intelligent agent (through a blind, unguided process that would occur in nature)? As you can see, if they cannot create new **kinds** through 60,000 generations of micro-evolution aided by intelligent minds, then macro-evolution in nature is almost certainly false.

We have another layer of refutation for macro-evolution:

The Fossil Record

If macro-evolution were true, we would see transitional life forms in the fossil record. But the fossil record is essentially devoid of transitional life forms. In fact, the fossil record seems to refute macro-evolution. If macro-evolution were true, we would see a gradual appearance of new body plans slowly throughout the history of life.

Think about this illustration: condense the entire history of the earth down into one hour. In the evolutionary model, at some point in that day, the self-replicating, single-celled organism would appear. Then, about every minute thereafter you would see a new life form appear in gradual succession through a slow process of micro-evolution.

What does the actual fossil record show us?

The complete opposite.

This is what the actual fossil record indicates: using the same illustration, condense the entire history of the earth down into one hour. Within a period of five seconds (**NOT** FIVE minutes, but FIVE **SECONDS**), all of the major body plans suddenly appear completely built and without preexisting transitional life forms. This period of time is what scientists call "The Cambrian Explosion." This refers to the era in history when the major phyla explode into existence seemingly out of nowhere. For macro-evolution to be true, there would be a gradual appearance of life forms over the history of life. But the evidence from the fossil record is that all of the major body plans burst into existence without precursors within a very short period of time. This fact disproves macro-evolution.[67]

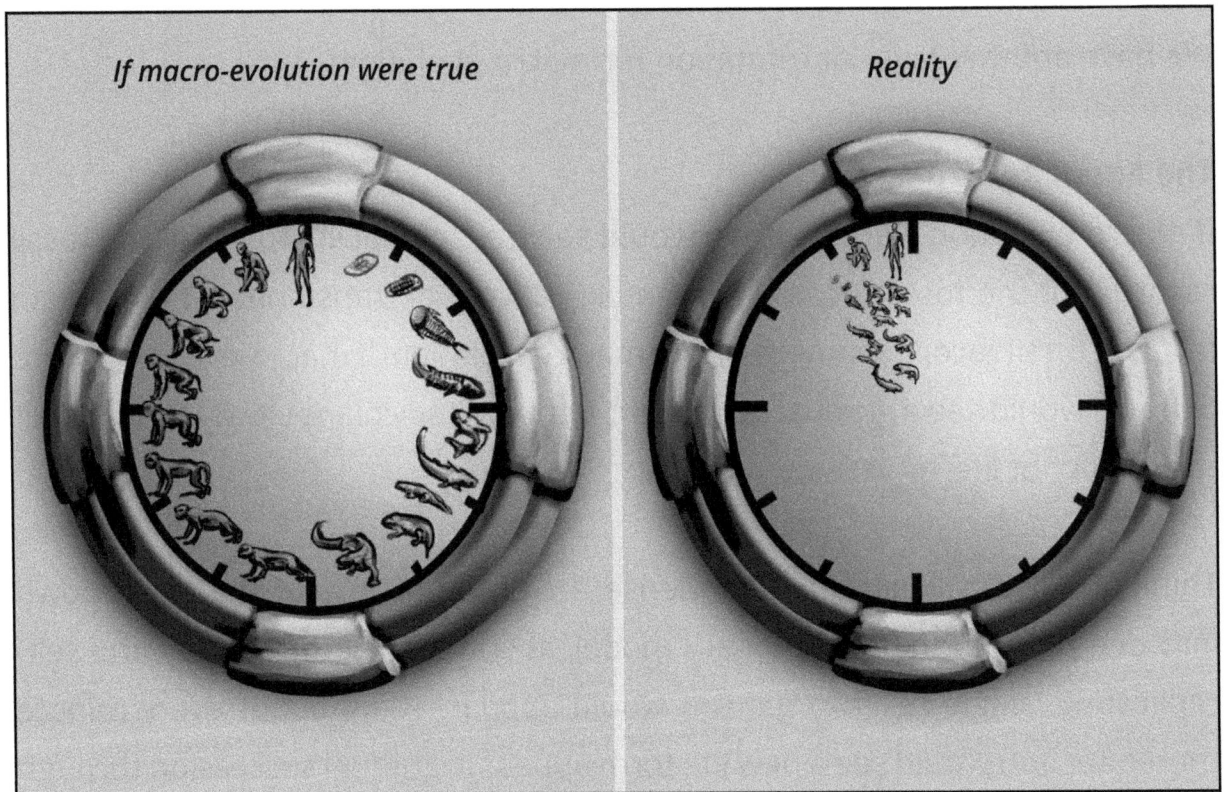

These clocks represent the entire history of the earth condensed down into one hour. If macro-evolution were true, then the fossil record would be represented by the clock on the left, which indicates a gradual descent of body plans over the course of time. Conversely, the true fossil record is represented by the clock on the right. Almost all of the major body plans are built out in a span of five seconds! I realize the clock on the right shows the body plans in five minutes rather than five seconds, but you get the idea.

Now, we have demonstrated through the long-term evolutionary experiments (fruit flies and E. coli) and the fossil record that **macro-evolution is false**. But for the sake of argument, let's suppose macro-evolution is true. The evolutionist would still have an enormous problem: the first self-replicating, single-celled organism. Where did that come from? If there was no life prior to this organism, how could it come into existence through evolution since there are no advantageous traits to select? This is called the "origin of the first life" problem. Evolutionists do not have a cogent framework to explain the origin of the first life (let alone any subsequent new life forms).

To summarize, when confronting the objection of evolution we ask a question:

What do you mean by evolution? **Do you mean <u>micro-evolution</u> or <u>macro-evolution</u>?**

Once we have asked these questions, we can use the evidence in the fossil record and the long-term evolutionary experiments to demonstrate that **macro-evolution is false**.

One reason otherwise brilliant biologists cling to macro-evolution is they are loyal to materialism prior to examining the evidence.

What is materialism?

In the next chapter, we will explore the objection:

"Everything that exists is made of materials."

CHAPTER 13

WHAT ABOUT MATERIALISM?

In this specific article, we will explore the topic of **materialism**. We are not talking about "materialism" in the sense of someone who places too much value in material possessions. We are not talking about someone with a shopping addiction. The "materialism" that we are going to examine in this chapter is the contention that all that exists is ultimately made of physical materials. This viewpoint is also called "physicalism" or "naturalism." In this chapter, we will use the term **materialism**.

During our apologetics interactions, materialism itself doesn't always arise as a specified objection, but rather materialism is a critical component of the atheist worldview. A materialist contends that everything that exists is made of matter. Everything that exists is made of some part of the periodic table of elements or the particles that form the elements in the table. Even all mental phenomena including thought, reason, and consciousness can be explained through physical interactions of matter in the brain.

In the previous chapter on evolution, we learned how proponents of the evolutionary theory believe new kinds arise from other forms despite the evidence to the contrary. Otherwise brilliant biologists cling to macro-evolution because they are loyal to materialism prior to examining the evidence. Indeed, an atheist is committed to materialism, and that position is fairly simple to understand: **All that exists is made of materials.**

The best way to handle this objection is to provide several examples of things that truly exist, but are **not** made of materials.

Here is a list of several undeniable realities that are **immaterial**:

The Laws of Mathematics

The Oxford English Dictionary definition of mathematics is "the abstract science which investigates deductively the conclusions implicit in the elementary conceptions of spatial and numerical relations, and which includes as its main divisions geometry, arithmetic, and algebra."[68] This definition itself posits that math is abstract—which means math is not made of materials. The easiest way to illustrate this is by using simple arithmetic. According to the Laws of Mathematics, it is true that 2+2=4. This is an objective law. It is true at all times and in all places. Even for a person who cannot sense tactile objects (blind/deaf/no sense of touch) 2+2=4 is true. It is a law.

How much mass does this law have? How much does it weigh? Which elements or particles is it made of? These questions don't make sense because it's obvious that the law is not made of anything. But it truly exists. The Laws of Mathematics are **immaterial**.

The Laws of Logic

We covered the Laws of Logic in the second chapter of this book. These laws are inescapable realities. For example, when you cross the street and see a car approaching, you can think of two possibilities: a car is coming, or a car is not coming. The Law of Non-Contradiction holds that these two propositions cannot be true at the same time and in the same sense. Maybe you don't know it, but you are acting in accordance with this law when you see the car coming, and you do not cross the street. It's so embedded into your mind that you don't even question it. Literally, many times per day you are accessing the Laws of

This illustration represents the mathematical law of 2+2=4 as made of stone.
But that law is not made of stone. It's not made of any material, but it does truly exist.
It just can't be weighed. It's immaterial.

Logic and acting on them. In fact, you can't even communicate with another person properly without both people accessing the same set of logical laws. How much mass do these laws have? How much do they weigh? Which elements or particles are they made of? These questions don't make sense because it's obvious that these laws are not made of anything. But they truly exist.

Someone might claim that the Laws of Logic are "human invention."

Here is an illustration to refute that claim: imagine the time in history before any humans existed. At that time, was the statement, *"No humans exist"* true? **Yes**! That statement was true, but no humans existed yet to invent the Laws of

Logic! Therefore, humans could not have invented the Laws of Logic, and they are not made of materials. The Laws of Logic are **immaterial**.[69]

Morality

We covered the fact that objective moral laws exist in Chapter 6. But they are not made of materials. It is true at all times and in all places that the Nazi human experiments were wrong. Therefore, these objective Laws of Morality truly exist.

How much mass do these laws have? How much do they weigh? Which elements or particles are they made of? These questions don't make sense because it's obvious that these laws are not made of anything. Objective moral laws are **immaterial**.

Aesthetical Judgments

Have you ever heard the saying, *"Beauty is in the eye of the beholder"*? This slogan points to the notion that people have different tastes. People have disparate preferences as to what they consider beautiful. Some people think rock music is beautiful. Some think rap music is beautiful. Some think poetry is beautiful. Some think ballet is beautiful. Some think a certain person is beautiful. Although people have different preferences as to what they consider beautiful, everyone thinks **something** is beautiful.

How much mass does beauty have? How much does it weigh? Which particles or elements build beauty? These questions don't make sense because it's obvious that beauty is not always made of anything. Beauty can be **immaterial**.[70]

As a side point, I would argue that **objective** beauty exists. I would refute the maxim, *"Beauty is in the eye of the beholder"* by submitting that a sunset over an ocean is truly more beautiful than a heaping garbage dump. Regarding sound, I would submit that Mozart's "Requiem" is more beautiful than a jackhammer endlessly pounding concrete. Would anyone argue with me? Notwithstanding, I will stick to my main point: beauty truly exists and it is not always made of materials.

Thoughts

I am a man. *Ich bin ein Mann*. In case you can't read German, *Ich bin ein Mann* means "I am a man." These two sentences identify the same "thought," but these words on this paper are **not** composed of the same materials. The letters are different, but they "say" the same thing (I am a man). Another way to see this phenomenon is to verbally say the following words separately: "I am a man" and "Ich bin ein Mann." You are saying the same "thing," but the composition of the sound emanating from your mouth is different. The frequencies of the verbal words are different, but they identify the same "thought." This means that the "thought" truly exists, but it is not made of materials.[71]

Another way to prove that a "thought" truly exists is by the placebo effect. The placebo effect occurs when someone is suffering from an affliction. This person ingests an inert pill, which, based on its own properties, has no effect on the physical body. However, if the person possesses the "thought" that the pill will have an effect, then that "thought" can produce a physical, bodily effect even though the pill does **not** contain such a property. In other words, something **immaterial** (a thought) can produce a **material** effect (change in body chemistry). This proves that thoughts exist.

Someone might claim that, "Thoughts are just products of brain chemistry."

Here is an illustration to refute that claim: Right now, think about a giant tree. Visualize it. Think of a tree. If a neurosurgeon physically examined your brain, would he discover a tree inside your skull? **No**! The physical materials that constitute the tree are not located in your brain. Conversely, the "thought" of the tree exists in your mind. Using instruments, neurosurgeons can detect activity in your brain **in response** to thoughts. During these observations, the researchers and the subjects interact. Sometimes, the researcher will ask the subject, "What are you thinking about?" Or the researcher will tell the subject to think about something. In response to the subject thinking, areas of the brain will be activated. This does not prove thoughts are just products of brain chemistry. This simply demonstrates that certain areas of the brain are activated by thoughts. The researcher will never find the material object that corresponds to the thought in the subject's brain.[72] Thoughts are **immaterial**.

Consequences of Materialism

Just for the sake of argument, let's assume atheism is true. Let's assume that all that exists is made of materials. This means that **you are simply a sentient sack of meat and bones**. All of your thoughts and feelings are simply reactions of chemical processes in your brain. All of your actions are the product of the atomic momentum of this universe. Since your behavior is determined by blind molecular interaction, how can you be held accountable for your actions?

If materialism is true, then you cannot be culpable for anything. You can kill someone and say, "It was just a product of chemical reactions in my brain." You are completely blameless because you are simply an automated collection of matter. Your actions are beyond your control, so it wouldn't be "just" to punish you for those actions. In fact, justice itself would not exist if materialism is true because justice is not made of materials. How much mass does justice have? How much does justice weigh? What are the particles and elements that build justice? Justice itself is **immaterial**.

If materialism is true, then you have no **reason** to think **anything** is true. Reason depends on the Laws of Logic. But the Laws of Logic are not made of materials so they would not exist if materialism is true. If the Laws of Logic do not exist, then reason does not exist because the process of reasoning relies on those fundamental laws. This is the great irony of atheism. Atheists claim to be "reasonable." Atheists claim to be champions of "reason." But reason itself would not exist if atheism (materialism) is true because reason is not made of materials!

If materialism is true, then your sense of identity is simply an artifact created by an assembly of cellular functions. Your consciousness is manufactured by a network of particle reactions. This means you are no more than a cocktail of carbon meshed up with a bunch of other elements. You are just a blob of atoms. So is everyone else.

I see only two consequences to this conclusion. You can repress it and conform to societal conventions and be a seemingly productive member of civilization. However, **free will** is immaterial; therefore, having the **free will** to repress a conclusion would be impossible if materialism is true!

So, the only outcome to consistently fastening yourself to materialism is to embrace your molecular machinery. Simply satisfy and gratify every urge you receive despite the impact on anyone else. A person is just a wet lump of tissue anyway, so a person doesn't really matter. If when you die, you truly cease to exist, then you should do whatever you want to do, despite anything or anyone else.

If everything is matter, <u>nothing matters</u>.

Luckily, based on the examples of abstract immaterial realities provided in this chapter, we have demonstrated that **materialism is false**.

In the next chapter, we will explore the objection:

"What about the Christian atrocities?"

CHAPTER 14

WHAT ABOUT THE CHRISTIAN ATROCITIES?

The first step to responding to an objection is to **ask a question**. The question should compel the objector to elaborate on his contention. You will find that the person usually doesn't have any evidence. He will simply repeat or rephrase his original catchphrase.

For example, someone might say, "What about all the Christian atrocities"? Or, "What about the Crusades? What about the Inquisition?" Or, "What about all the killings in the name of Christ?"

How do you respond?

You should **not** respond by saying that those atrocities happened hundreds of years ago. As we discussed in Chapter 6, objective moral laws exist. Therefore, certain actions are wrong at all times and in all places, including atrocities of centuries ago.

This is the right response: You should ask, "<u>**Do those atrocities prove that Christianity is false?**</u>"

Even if you grant that the objection is correct that there have been Christian atrocities or killings in the name of Christ, this assertion does not prove Christianity is false. The fact that self-identifying "Christians" have committed atrocities does not mean that Christianity is false. Despite these atrocities, Jesus still could have been crucified and risen from the dead. In fact, the question of Christian atrocities is a great way to spread the gospel. How so?

Christian Atrocities Illuminate the Need for a Savior

Christianity teaches that everyone, including Christians, are sinful by nature. Humans are bent toward poor behavior. That statement embodies an integral component of the Christian worldview. If Christianity is true, we would expect to find Christians committing sins. Therefore, ironically, the Christian atrocities actually help to confirm that Christianity is true by demonstrating that everyone is sinful. From here we can explain why Jesus took on human flesh: to expiate the atrocities committed by everyone, including Christians.

Now let's examine the truth of the Christian atrocity objection:

Atrocities by the Numbers

The historical developments of the Crusades and the Inquisition, or any other "Christian war" or "Christian violence," will usually highlight how these "atrocities" do not involve true Christianity. Most people do not have an accurate understanding of the perpetrators' motivations driving these events. Most people are surprised to learn that many of these episodes had nothing to do with Christianity. But, due to the limited space in this book, let's leave that to the side.

Let's look at the number of atrocities committed by atheists versus the number of atrocities committed by "Christians":

Atheist Atrocity	Death Toll	Christian Atrocity	Death Toll
Mao Zedong, China, 1958–1961: The Great Leap Forward	18-70 Million	30 Years' War, Europe: 1618–1648	3-11 Million
Lenin and Stalin, USSR, 1917–1953: Russian Civil War and the Purges	9-30 Million	French Wars of Religion, France: 1562–1598	2-4 Million
*Hitler, Germany/ Europe, 1933–1945: The Holocaust	4-6 Million	100 Years' War Europe: 1337–1453	2-3 Million
Pol Pot, Cambodia, 1975–1979: Khmer Rouge "Killing Fields"	1-3 Million	Combined Crusades, Middle East: 1095-1291	1-3 Million
Kim Il Sung, Korea, 1949–1994: Various Mass Murders	1-2 Million	The Inquisition, Spanish Empire: 1478–1834	150-300 Thousand
Mussolini, Italy, 1936–1945: Persecution under Regime	300 Thousand	The Troubles, Ireland/England: 1968–1998	3-4 Thousand
Total Death Toll by Atheist Atrocities	**33-111 Million**	**Total Death Toll by Christian Atrocities**	**8-21 Million**

*Do not let anyone tell you that Hitler was a Christian. He willfully rejected his baptism. Hitler only invoked God in his public speeches to gain the trust of the German people. For Hitler the word "God" was simply a political tool. Germany had been a deeply religious culture for centuries prior to the rise of the Nazis. Hitler concluded that the people would not condone his message and extermination programs unless he appealed to a "creator." His religious language was misdirection. It was a "front" for the mass audience. If you read Hitler's private correspondences and his henchmen's journals, it's abundantly clear that the Nazi regimes' long-term goal was to eradicate religion. He constantly referred to Christianity as a "scourge" or "the decay." Hitler was a hardcore social Darwinist who was fiercely devoted to evolution by natural selection. That was part of his rationale for systematically annihilating the "undesirables." In Hitler's view, he was aiding and expediting the evolutionary process to create a super race.[73,74,75,76,77,78,79,80,81,82]

As we see on the chart,[83] the atrocities committed in the name of atheism far surpass the atrocities committed in the name of Christ. This chart could look much worse for the atheists. In the atheist column, I omitted the total death toll of the wars in which the atheist players were involved. I only included deaths resulting from their individual actions and approvals. Conversely, in the Christian column, I included the total death toll of the "Christian" wars. Furthermore, the atheist column spans less than one hundred years whereas the Christian column spans almost four hundred! And the atheist atrocities still overwhelmingly exceed the Christian atrocities.

All that being said, atheist atrocities do not prove that atheism is false just as the alleged "Christian atrocities" do not prove that Christianity is false.

In order to defend Christianity against the "atrocity" objection, we simply cite what the New Testament teaches about violence.

New Testament Declarations on Violence
An effective response to the "atrocity" objection is to enlighten the objector on what the New Testament teaches about violence. Following is a list of relevant Scripture:

Luke 6:27–29 – "Love your enemies, do good to those who hate you, bless those who curse you, pray for those who abuse you. To one who strikes you on the cheek, offer the other also, and from one who takes away your cloak do not withhold your tunic either."

Matthew 5:9 – "Blessed are the peacemakers, for they will be called sons of God."

Matthew 5:39 – "But if anyone slaps you on the right cheek, turn to him the other cheek also."

Matthew 5:44 – "Love your enemies and pray for those who persecute you."

Matthew 26:52 – "All who take the sword will perish by the sword."

Mark 9:50 – "Be at peace with one another."

Romans 12:17 – "Repay no one evil for evil."

Romans 12:21 – "Do not be overcome by evil, but overcome evil with good."

Romans 14:19 – "So then let us pursue what makes for peace and for mutual up-building."

1 Corinthians 7:15 – "God has called us to live in peace."

Hebrews 12:14 – "Strive for peace with everyone"

James 3:18 – "A harvest of righteousness is sown in peace by those who make peace."

1 Peter 3:11 – "Let him turn away from evil and do good; let him seek peace and pursue it."

1 Thessalonians 5:15 – "See that no one repays anyone evil for evil, but always seek to do good to one another and to everyone."

The New Testament is replete with declarations of nonviolence. Given this undeniable fact embedded in the Scripture above, we can demonstrate that the perpetrators of the Christian atrocities were not acting in alignment with the instructions of Christianity. The culprits were committing actions completely **contradictory** to what Christianity teaches.

What about the Old Testament?

After sharing how the New Testament explicitly condemns violence, some people may refer to what they consider an atrocity in the Old Testament.

Again, we can take this opportunity to spread the gospel: we can explain how Jesus Christ has fulfilled the Old Testament Law. The unique prescriptions to eradicate sin in the Old Testament were precisely and exclusively aimed at specific populations. These directions do not apply to present-day people because we are fulfilled in Christ.

What about the slaughter of the Canaanites?

The most common example of an Old Testament atrocity is the slaughter of the Canaanites.

Someone might ask, "How can a loving God command the slaughter Canaanites?"

The response: **the Canaanites were purveyors of utter evil**. In addition to pervasive beatings, torture, and cult killings, the Canaanites engaged in polygamy, adultery, incest, bestiality, and ritual sex orgies. If that wasn't enough to justify wiping them out, the Canaanites sacrificed children to their god Moloch.[85] Yes, the Canaanites murdered their own sons and daughters.

The Canaanites fashioned a giant metal idol in the form of an anthropomorphic bull, which was an effigy to their god Moloch. The bull was positioned so that his "arms" were extended to where his "hands" created an altar that was glazed in bronze. The Canaanites would ignite a fire to super-heat the statue. Then, they would place their own children on the molten hot platform. At this point the children were slowly seared alive in the most excruciating pain imaginable on the smelted slab of bronze metal. The children would cry so loud that the "acolytes" would beat their drums in an effort to drown out the blood-curdling screams from the children—the children who were burning to death. The Canaanites scorched to death their own sons and daughters.

Now that we know this, was our God, the true God, justified in eliminating the sin of the Canaanites?

Of course!

Artist rendering of Moloch

The "Christian atrocity" objection does not prove Christianity is false. Furthermore, based on sheer death toll, atheists have committed far more atrocities than Christians. However, the most effective method of handling the "Christian atrocity" objection is by sharing the true teachings of Christianity and how the culprits were not acting in accordance with it.

In the next chapter, we will explore the objection:

"Why does God allow suffering?"

CHAPTER 15

WHY DOES GOD ALLOW SUFFERING?

We have presented a positive case for Christianity in Chapters 1 through 11. Now we will need to know how to effectively navigate common objections to Christianity. Oftentimes, our opportunity to defend Christianity arises from an objection. That is, rather than having the chance to present a positive case using the framework provided in this book, we are obliged to respond to someone who regurgitates a fictitious slogan. This person is issuing an objection to Christianity. From my experience, this person probably has not examined his own objection. He might be repeating a catchy sound bite. In this chapter, I will write about how to respond to a common objection.

One such objection is:

"I can't believe in God because why would a God who loves all His creatures allow them to suffer if He has the power to stop it?" Or, "Why does God allow child abuse?" Or, "Why does God allow people to die of cancer?" Or, "Why does God allow tsunamis and floods, killing thousands of people?"

All of these questions fall under the same general objection:

Why does God allow suffering?

The first step to responding to this objection is to **ask a question**.

The question:

"What do you mean by suffering?"

The purpose of this question is to draw the distinction between two different kinds of suffering. This distinction will help us navigate the objection.

Suffering at the hands of another individual is the first kind of suffering. Examples of this kind of suffering are theft, rape, murder, or any other evil committed by one person that directly causes the suffering of another person. This kind of suffering is otherwise known as **evil**.

One method of handling the objection of evil is by leveraging the evidence in Chapter 6 of this book (objective moral laws). If God does not exist, then there is no objective foundation for good, and without a standard of good, then we cannot define evil. We can call something evil only if we can measure it against an unchanging standard of good.[86] If God does not exist, then "good" is simply a matter of opinion. If God does not exist, then one person can define the Nazis as evil, but Hitler can define them as good. There would be no objective definition of evil if God does not exist. Therefore, if a person can identify something as objective evil, then he is actually admitting that God does exist. By using this line of reasoning (objective moral laws in Chapter 6), the evil objection is shattered. However, there are other ways to defeat the evil objection.

"Why does God allow evil if he has the power to stop it?"

If God were to stop evil, He would probably have to start with **you and me**.[87] Yes, you and I commit evil that causes other people to suffer. So if God wanted to stop evil to prevent suffering, then He would essentially have to eliminate everyone from existence because everyone causes suffering.

Recall the Canaanites from Chapter 14. They were committing evil acts by sacrificing their own children by burning them alive on an altar to a false god, Moloch. Obviously, this was causing their innocent children to suffer. God tried to stop this suffering by commanding the extermination of the Canaanites. And when He attempted to stop this evil, the objector begrudged Him for it.

In one breath the objector will ask, "Why did God command the slaughter of the Canaanites?"

And in the next breath the objector will ask, "Why doesn't God stop evil?"

To this objector I say: God tried to stop evil by annihilating the Canaanites, and you had a problem with it. So which route do you want Him to go? Do you want Him to leave everyone alone or do you want Him to stop evil? You can't have it both ways.

This is where we arrive at the best way to answer the objection, "Why does God allow evil?"

Free will.

The most effective answer to the question of suffering at the hands of another individual (evil) is the concept of free will. God gives us free will in our daily affairs. The reason God gave us free will is because He wants us to love each other. In order to love your neighbor as yourself, you must freely choose to do it; otherwise, it's not really love. Love, by definition, must be freely given.

Think about someone you love. Did this person **force** you to love him or do you love him of your own free will? Could anyone **force** you to love him? If someone said, "I will convince you to love me," would you listen and instantly love him? **No**! Love doesn't work like that. Any forced affection is simply compulsory compliance. It's not really love. Love requires free will. Now, since free will exists, evil exists because some people will inevitably use their free will for evil rather than love. And this evil causes suffering.

In summary, God gave us the possibility of love, and where there is the possibly of love, there is the reality of free will, and where there is free will, there will be evil in this world.

Okay. Now on to the other kind of suffering. I will call this suffering **natural suffering**. This kind of suffering doesn't seem to be caused by another individual. Examples of this kind of suffering are tsunamis, floods, earthquakes, pediatric cancer, Alzheimer's disease, etc. Another example of natural suffering is a church roof collapsing on a group of people worshipping the very God who is supposed to love them.

This kind of suffering is perhaps the most difficult objection to navigate because an intellectual answer is not always sufficient. Sure, we can provide data about how natural disasters are necessary for life to exist (see Chapter 4). We can provide data that some undeserved diseases are a result of free-will, unhealthy choices. We can provide data that some buildings are poorly constructed or erected in areas where they shouldn't be built. But all of these explanations miss the mark.

To the question of suffering, people crave an emotional answer rather than a purely intellectual answer. An effective response is telling a story from your own personal experience with suffering.

Here is mine:

My mom has big teeth. My dad has a small mouth. During the formation of my body, my DNA communicated a message that gave me my mom's teeth and my dad's mouth. Thanks a lot, DNA! Actually, as we covered in Chapter 5, messages only come from intelligent minds, which in this case points to God, so I can blame Him!

Anyway, when I was ten years old, it was determined that my mouth would not fit my teeth, so I was forced to undergo a battery of orthodontic procedures. One such procedure was the installation of a "rapid maxillary expansion appliance" or "palate expander." I called it the "Jaw Breaker." This device was affixed to my molars with a web of aluminum arching along the roof of my mouth. The heat from my mouth was supposed to slowly expand the metal, which would force my upper jaw to widen outwardly and create room for my teeth. There is a deficiency with this appliance. When installed in a mouth breather, the heat escapes the mouth prior to warming the metal sufficiently enough to expand the jaw. The alternative is a mechanical palate expander in which someone has to go into the mouth with a key and crank a gear that would forcibly expand the metal, which in turn would widen the jaw.

After a year of the Jaw Breaker's torment, I had to endure standard braces for two years and then a retainer for several more years thereafter. This entire process was painful. My teeth were always sore. My mouth was extremely hard to clean, so it was often infected. My gums were sliced and irritated by the bands of metal. The roof of my mouth was slowly cracked open so it would broaden out. I had speech problems. I had trouble swallowing, which caused excessive salivation. Not to mention that when I smiled, it looked like I had a scrap yard in my mouth, which was the target of ridicule from my peers.

My parents had the power to stop it. They could've stopped paying the dentist. They could have told the dentist to take it all out. My parents were supposed to love me, but they allowed me to suffer even though they had the power to stop it. Was this a good reason to say that my parents did not exist? **Of course not!** Just because my parents allowed me to suffer doesn't mean that my parents don't exist! In the same manner, just because God allows us to suffer doesn't mean that He does not exist.

Furthermore, before my parents chose to have children, they knew for a fact that their children would suffer. But they chose to have children anyway. Suffering is inevitable in life, but that didn't stop my parents from having children and that doesn't mean they don't love me. The same is true with God. He knows that we will suffer in life, but He chose to create us anyway. It doesn't prove that He doesn't love us, and it certainly doesn't prove that He does not exist. Given this analogy, the "Why does God allow suffering?" objection is muted.

But let's go one step further.

Why did my parents, who love me, allow me to suffer even though they had the power to stop it? Why did my parents allow suffering?

They tried to tell me. They gave me the intellectual answers. They told me that crooked teeth can cause issues with my gums, tooth decay, recurring infections, and breathing problems. "The mouth is the gateway to the body," they said.

I still didn't buy it.

I still wanted to know: If they loved me, why would they allow me to suffer when they had the power to stop it?

They tried a different approach. They told me that straightening my teeth would give me a beautiful smile, which I will appreciate "**later in life**."

And now we arrive at the crux of the problem of suffering.

As a child, I was "stuck" in a limited perspective of time. I wasn't concerned about the long run. I couldn't see "**later in life**." I couldn't see the positive **future** effects of **present** suffering because I was limited by time. But my parents, having a different perspective of time, were able to see that if they allowed me to suffer in the **present**, I would be better in the **future**. And they allowed me to suffer precisely because they loved me.

The same is true for why God allows suffering. We humans cannot see beyond our line of sight. We cannot see the long run. We do not see the ultimate outcome of our suffering. We are "stuck" in the limited perspective of time itself. We are restricted to the dimension of time, which limits our understanding of suffering.

But as we covered in Chapter 3 (beginning of the universe), God exists independently of our notion of time. He is not confined by the limits of time like you and me. He sees how suffering ultimately enables good. He sees that allowing **present** suffering empowers us to be better in the **future**. And He allows us to suffer precisely because He loves us.

When you hang a picture or decoration on a wall in your home, you always take a few steps away from the wall so that you can see if the item is level. If you are right up close to the wall, you cannot tell if it hangs true. You need a remote perspective outside of your current limitations. God has this outside perspective because he exists outside of our universe. He sees how our suffering can improve our character.

In this illustration, the mirror represents "time." As limited human beings, we are confined by the current dimension of time. We cannot see the beautiful valley that lies ahead.
We can only see our present suffering and remember our past struggles.
Conversely, God sees the entire "picture," so He allows the wolves and the thorns to bedevil us because He knows that a gorgeous setting awaits.

God allows us to struggle so that we can be resilient. He allows us to encounter danger so that we can be brave. He allows us to have pain so that we can know healing. He allows us to have hardships, so that we can have strength. He allows us to suffer in this world so that we can have everlasting joy in the next.

In the next chapter, we will explore the objection:

"Why would God send me to hell?"

CHAPTER 16

WHY WOULD GOD SEND ME TO HELL?

Another objection from someone who regurgitates a fictitious slogan is:

"I can't believe in God because why would a loving God send me to hell?"

The first step to responding to this objection is to **ask a question**.

The question:

"What do you mean by hell?"

The purpose of this question is to ascertain the objector's perception of hell. This understanding will help us navigate the objection.

Most people think hell is a place where the devil chains you to a rock and stabs you with a pitchfork all day. This, and related images of hell, are faulty because they are expressing an element of torture. However, hell is not described as torturous per se, but rather hell is a place of **torment**. Torment is different than torture. Torture is someone actively inflicting pain on another person for pleasure or for some other purpose serving the torturer. Torment is constant misery or anguish.

Knowing this distinction, you can clarify the nature of hell. Hell is simply **separation** from God's goodness. If you are in hell, you are not continually gored with the Devil's horns or whipped with his tail or stomped by his hoofs. No. Forget all that. Hell is where you are **separated** from God's grace. And, if you are in hell, this is exactly what you want. If you go through life actively rejecting God, separating yourself from His gifts, then this is the exact type of existence He gives you for eternity. He gives you what you want.

The opposite of hell is heaven. Heaven is eternal life in the presence of and in fellowship with God, where your attention and free will is rightly directed toward Him. If you actively reject this brand of life on earth, then God will allow that rejection to perpetuate for eternity (hell).

I would like for you to be my friend. I tell you this on a daily basis. You do not reciprocate. I email you. You ignore me. I call you. You disregard me. I text you. You snub me. I invite you for supper at my house. You flout me. I ask you to come over for a swim in the pool. You rebuff me. I keep bidding for your companionship. Now you are annoyed. Every time I summon your fellowship, you rebuke me. Can't I take a hint? Why don't I understand? You don't have interest in any relationship with me. You don't want anything to do with me. Finally, it's time for my wedding, where all the attention and will is rightly directed at me. I send you an official invitation to attend my wedding. You actively reject the invitation. You do not want to be in a place where I am glorified. Your heart is against me.

Knowing your heart, should I force you to attend my wedding against your will? Should I bound you in shackles and drag you into my presence, even though you do not want anything to do with me?

No!

It would be **unloving** for me to force you into my glory.

What is the **loving** thing to do in this situation?

Allow you to go your own way. Allow you to go to a place where you are **separated** from me. After trying over and over again, I know your heart and how much you don't want me; therefore, it is **loving** to let you go into estrangement with me.

And this is exactly what God does to those in hell. God invites them into a relationship with Him, and they actively reject Him. They do not want to be in a place where God is eternally and universally glorified (heaven), and after this constant dismissal and outright repudiation, God, **because he is loving**, gives them what they want (hell). Very simply, hell is another partition of reality that God created to **separate** those who do not want Him.

Another similar objection is, **"I can't accept Christianity because it's an exclusive religion."** This is what I call the "exclusivity" objection. The objector is contending that because Christianity excludes other religions, he cannot accept it.

Firstly, just because Christianity is exclusive doesn't mean that it's not true. You shouldn't accept something on the basis of whether or not it's exclusive, but rather you should accept things based on whether or not they are true.

Secondly, this objection violates the Law of Noncontradiction, so it is false. The objector is saying Christianity is unacceptable because it excludes other religions; however, his own claim excludes Christianity, so by his own standard that claim is unacceptable because it excludes other religions (Christianity). The objection is a self-defeating position.

Thirdly, every single religion is "exclusive" because all religions make directly contradictory truth claims.[88] For example, atheism, agnosticism, Buddhism, and certain other eastern philosophies posit that God does not exist. Hinduism proposes that many deities once existed, but that now "everything" is God. Judaism, Islam, and Christianity hold that only one God exists, but each disagrees on the nature of Jesus. Judaism says He was a false teacher, and Islam regards Him as a mere prophet. Differentially, Christianity pronounces that Jesus is God.

Which brings us to another objection: **how can Jesus be the only way?**

Jesus is the only way because, as we have demonstrated in this chapter, if you vigorously renounce Jesus in this world, then He will grant your request to live in separation from Him for eternity (hell).

Also, all sin came into the world through one man (Adam in the Garden of Eden); therefore, all sin is redeemed through one man—Jesus.

Most importantly, Jesus Himself repeatedly specified that **He is the only way**.

New Testament declarations that Jesus is the Only Way

An effective response to the "exclusivity" objection is to enlighten the objector on what the New Testament teaches about how Jesus is the only way. Below is a list of relevant Scripture:

John 14:6 – Jesus said, "I am the way, and the truth, and the life. No one comes to the Father except through me."

John 8:24 – Jesus said, "I told you that you would die in your sins, for unless you believe that I am He you will die in your sins."

John 10:9 – Jesus said, "I am the door. If anyone enters by me, he will be saved and will go in and out and find pasture."

John 8:12 – Jesus said, "I am the light of the world. Whoever follows me will not walk in darkness, but will have the light of life."

John 10:7, 10:1 – Jesus said, "I am the gate for the sheep ... anyone who does not enter the sheep pen by the gate, but climbs in by some other way, is a thief and a robber."

John 15:6 – Jesus said, "If anyone does not abide in me he is thrown away like a branch and withers; and the branches are gathered, thrown into the fire, and burned."

John 11:25 – Jesus said, "I am the resurrection and the life. Whoever believes in me, though he die, yet shall he live, and everyone who lives and believes in me shall never die."

Acts 4:12 – "And there is salvation in no one else [except Jesus], for there is no other name under heaven given among men by which we must be saved."

1 Timothy 2:5 – "For there is one God, and there is one mediator between God and men, the man Christ Jesus."

Matthew 20:28 – Jesus said, "Even as the Son of Man came not to be served but to serve, and to give His life as a ransom for many."

2 Corinthians 5:21 – "For our sake he made Him to be sin who knew no sin, so that in Him we might become the righteousness of God."

John 3:16 – "For God so loved the world that he gave his only Son, that whoever believes in him should not perish but have eternal life."

The New Testament is replete with declarations that, yes, Jesus is the only way to heaven. Anyone who actively rejects Him will receive what he wants for eternity—**separation** from Jesus (hell).

In the next chapter, we will reaffirm:

"Why should a Christian do apologetics?"

If someone spends his whole life shaking his fist at God, rejecting His grace, then God will grant him that existence into what we call "hell." God quarantines and separates the eschewer who continues to reject God throughout eternity.

CHAPTER 17

WHY SHOULD A CHRISTIAN DO APOLOGETICS?

In the first chapter, I challenged you with the following question:

If someone were to ask, "**Why do you believe in God?**" what would you tell him?

Think about it for a second. How would you respond to that question?

Hopefully, after reading sixteen chapters of this book, you have sufficient ammunition to respond to that question and defend your faith. The evidence that Christianity is true is vast and exhaustive. Christianity seems to be true beyond reasonable doubt.

So why are there so many smart people who are not Christian?

Before we answer that, let me remind you that if you are a Christian, you are commanded to do apologetics.

Here is specific Scripture supporting the apologetics calling (bold added for emphasis):

1 Peter 3:15 – "In your hearts honor Christ the Lord as holy, **always being prepared to make a defense to anyone who asks you for a reason for the hope that is in you**; yet do it with gentleness and respect."

2 Corinthians 10:5 – "**We destroy arguments and every lofty opinion raised against the knowledge of God**, and take every thought captive to obey Christ."

Jude 1:3 – "Beloved, although I was very eager to write to you about our common salvation, I found it necessary to write appealing to you to **contend for the faith** that was once for all delivered to the saints."

Philippians 1:7 – "It is right for me to feel this way about you all, because I hold you in my heart, for you are all partakers with me of grace, both in my imprisonment and in the **defense and confirmation of the gospel**."

Titus 1:9 – "He must hold firm to the trustworthy word as taught, so that he may be able to give instruction in sound doctrine and also to **rebuke those who contradict it**."

Matthew 10:32–33 – "So everyone who **acknowledges me before men**, I also will acknowledge before my Father who is in heaven, but whoever denies me before men, I also will deny before my Father who is in heaven."

Perhaps the most direct command for apologetics is the greatest commandment:

Mark 12:30 – (Jesus said) "And you shall love the Lord your God with all your heart and with all your soul and with all your **mind** and with all your strength."

In the greatest commandment (also found in Matthew and Luke), Jesus commands us to love him with the totality of our **mind**. Surely, our minds are designed by God to use reason and rationale. If we dive into our faith with our mind, our faith will be further enriched by God's precious Word and his magnificent creation.

Now, despite all of the evidence we've covered in this book, you cannot "argue someone into faith." God alone can endow faith through His means of grace. However, during the course of contending for Christianity (apologetics), perhaps God can provide faith to the person with whom you are speaking—the listener. (Romans 10:17 – "Faith comes through hearing.")

Even after you present a positive case that Christianity is true and effectively handle objections, this person still will not believe that Christianity is true.

So why are so many smart people not Christian?

The problem is with the **heart**, not the mind.

The evidence is not the issue.

Someone can possess all of the intellectual reasons of why Christianity is true but still reject the truth because this person does not **want** it to be true.[89]

Why would someone not want Christianity to be true?

Many people have a distorted perception of Christianity. Many people view God as a "sky tyrant." To these people, God is an arrogant autocrat perched on a throne in the clouds. To these people, God is an overbearing authority figure drilling people on rules and regulations. These people think that God is looking down on them and condemning them for every little thing that they do. Undoubtedly, like everyone else, these people are committing sins in their personal lives. And they think God hates them for it. So they are angry at God.

Rather than accepting the evidence that Christianity is true, they would rather deny it so they don't have to confront the consequence of the fact that God does exist. This avoidance and repudiation enables people to continue on their chosen paths without guilt.

Let me dismount from my high horse. It's very easy to deny something because we don't want it to be true. It almost seems like a component of the default human condition. It's a real problem for us, including me.

The way to address this problem is to understand the one true God. The oppressive god represented as a celestial despot is a false god. I do not believe in that god. That god does not exist.

The God of Christianity **does exist**.

The triune God loves us, so he provides a framework of behavior that will be **constructive** and not **destructive**. This is the reason for the "rules and regulations" He seems to impose.

Parents issue rules to their children. Why? Because parents love their children. If parents did not love their children, they would let them do whatever they want. Likewise, God loves us, so he gives us guidance on how to act in a way that will be beneficial to us. These "rules" are for our own good. These "rules" are grounded in God's character. God is the standard of good (see Chapter 6).

Can we, without God, possibly meet this standard?

NO.

Every single one of us has fallen short. And since God is infinitely just, He must issue a penalty for this shortfall.

But it's impossible to reach this standard on our own, so what are we supposed to do?

God is not only infinitely just, He is infinitely loving and infinitely wise. So He developed a plan to account for our deficit.

What is the plan?

Simple. Look to the cross where God himself (**Jesus**) paid the penalty on our behalf.

We don't have to do any work on our own. Not only is our debt paid in full, Jesus takes it one step further and imputes his righteousness to us. Given the free gift of faith, God sees us through the lens of Christ's work, not our own.

This is not an arbitrary system of "rules and regulations." This is the most emancipating arrangement I can imagine. This is Christianity.

This explanation is an effective Christian apologetics strategy—a simple, yet profound overview of the gospel. You can make a stellar presentation of why Christianity is true and wade through seemingly endless objections, but sometimes, people just need to hear the Good News of redemption.

The opportunity to share the gospel usually emerges after you have developed a relationship with a person. Maybe a friend, coworker, or family member has resisted every hint you've dropped about why Christianity is true. Some might be openly hostile to Christianity.

Don't shun skeptics. Don't eschew agnostics. Don't evade atheists.

Don't deport opponents of Christianity from your lives.

Pray for them.

Then, one day you might get an email. You might get a text message. Your phone might ring.

The person says:

"Do you remember when you told me that everything that begins to exist has a cause? What did you mean by that?"

Or,

"Do you remember when you told me about the fine-tuning of the universe? What did you mean by that?"

Or,

"Do you remember when you told me about the message in DNA? What did you mean by that?"

Or,

"Do you remember when you told me about objective moral laws? What did you mean by that?"

Or,

"Do you remember when you told me that the New Testament is true? What did you mean by that?"

Or

"Do you remember when you told me that God paid the penalty for my shortfall? What did you mean by that?"

You're a Christian apologist now. I pray that you know how to respond.

GENERAL REFERENCES AND NOTES

1. All scriptural references are cited from: Engelbrecht, Edward. *The Lutheran Study Bible*: English Standard Version. Saint Louis: Concordia Publishing House, 2009.

2. Hagist, Don N. *British Soldiers, American War: Voices of the American Revolution*. Yardley, Pa.: Westholme, 2012.

3. Geist, Christopher. "A Common American Soldier." *Colonial Williamsburg Journal* Autumn 2004 (2004). Accessed April 21, 2015.

4. Geisler, Norman L., and Frank Turek. *I Don't Have Enough Faith to Be an Atheist*. Wheaton, Ill.: Crossway Books, 2004.

5. "Why You OUGHT to Judge" - Cross Examined - Christian Apologetic Ministry | Frank Turek | Christian Apologetics | Christian Apologetics Speakers." June 16, 2008. Accessed April 11, 2015. http://crossexamined.org/why-you-ought-to-judge/.

6. "Uranium Decay Data." WWW Table of Radioactive Isotopes. Accessed April 21, 2015. http://ie.lbl.gov/toi/nucSearch.asp.

7. Fontaine, G.; Brassard, P.; Bergeron, P. (2001). "The Potential of White Dwarf Cosmochronology". Publications of the Astronomical Society of the Pacific 113 (782): 409.

8. Guggenheim, Edward Armand. *Thermodynamics: An Advanced Treatment for Chemists and Physicists*. 6th ed. Amsterdam: North-Holland, 1977.

9. Penzias, A. A., and R. W. Wilson. "A Measurement of Excess Antenna Temperature At 4080 Mc/s." *Astrophysical Journal*, 419.

10. "Hitchens vs. Turek, Virginia Commonwealth University." Hitchens Debates Transcripts. November 9, 2010. Accessed April 21, 2015. http://hitchensdebates.blogspot.com/2010/11/hitchens-vs-turek-vcu.html.

11. Maas, Korey, and Adam Francisco. *Making the Case for Christianity: Responding to Modern Objections*. St. Louis: Concordia Publishing House, 2014.

12. "Is God a Delusion? - Sheldonian Theatre, Oxford." ReasonableFaith.org. October 24, 2011. Accessed April 21, 2015. http://www.reasonablefaith.org/media/is-god-a-delusion-sheldonian-theatre-oxford.

13. Lawrence M. Krauss, "The End of the Age Problem and the Case for a Cosmological Constant Revisited," *Astrophysical Journal* 501 (1998): 461-466.

14. Polkinghorne, J. C. *Science and Providence: God's Interaction with the World*. Templeton Foundation Press ed. Philadelphia: Templeton Foundation Press, 2005.

15. McGinn, Colin. *Basic Structures of Reality: Essays in Meta-physics*. New York: Oxford University Press, 2011.

16. Overman, Dean L. *A Case against Accident and Self-organization*. Lanham: Rowman & Littlefield, 1997.

17. "Milky Way Galaxy." University of Arizona. Accessed April 21, 2015. http://lithops.as.arizona.edu/~jill/EPO/Stars/galaxy.html.

18. Barrow, John D., and Joseph Silk. *The Left Hand of Creation: The Origin and Evolution of the Expanding Universe*. New York: Basic Books, 1983.

19. Ross, Hugh. *The Creator and the Cosmos: How the Greatest Scientific Discoveries of the Century Reveal God*. Colorado Springs, Colo.: NavPress, 1993.

20. Ibid.

21. Ibid.

22. Ibid.

23. Ibid.

24. S. W. Hawking, "Cosmology from the Top Down," paper presented at the Davis Cosmic Inflation Meeting, U. C. Davis, May 29, 2003.

25. Ross, Hugh. *The Creator and the Cosmos: How the Greatest Scientific Discoveries of the Century Reveal God*. Colorado Springs, Colo.: NavPress, 1993.

26. Sproul, R. C., and Keith A. Mathison. *Not a Chance: God, Science, and the Revolt against Reason*. Expanded ed.

27. Assuming a thickness of .0043 inches.

28. Alberts, Bruce. *Molecular Biology of the Cell*. 4th ed. New York: Garland Science, 2002.

29. Using my own calculations from Dawkins, Richard. *The Blind Watchmaker*. New York: Norton, 1986.

30. Department of Experimental, Diagnostic and Specialty Medicine. University of Bologna, Bologna, Italy.

31. Meyer, Stephen C. *Signature in the Cell: DNA and the Evidence for Intelligent Design*. New York: HarperOne, 2009.

32. Lagnado, Lucette, and Sheila Cohn Dekel. *Children of the Flames: Dr. Josef Mengele and the Untold Story of the Twins of Auschwitz*. New York: Morrow, 1990.

33. Lutzer, Erwin W. *When a Nation Forgets God: 7 Lessons We Must Learn from Nazi Germany*. Chicago: Moody Publishers, 2010.

34. Craig, William Lane. *Reasonable faith: Christian truth and Apologetics*. Wheaton, Ill.: Crossway Books, 2008.

35. Lewis, C. S. *Mere Christianity*. New York: Macmillan, 1958.

36. Hill, Benno. *Murderous Science: Elimination by Scientific Selection of Jews, Gypsies, and Others, Germany 1933–1945*. Oxfordshire: Oxford University Press, 1988.

37. Lennox, John C. *God's Undertaker: Has Science Buried God?* Updated ed. Oxford: Lion, 2009.

38. Turek, Frank. "TOP TEN REASONS WE KNOW THE NEW TESTAMENT IS TRUE." Lecture, 2011 Ahmanson Lectures on Apologetics, November 26, 2011.

39. Merriam-Webster Online Dictionary. Merriam-Webster, Inc. Retrieved 2015-04-22.

40. Geisler, Norman L. Baker. *Encyclopedia of Christian Apologetics*. Grand Rapids, Mich.: Baker Books, 1999.

41. McDowell, Josh. *New Evidence That Demands a Verdict*. [Rev., Updated, and Expanded]. ed. Nashville, Tenn.: Thomas Nelson, 1999.

42. Brumbaugh, Robert S. and Rulon S. Wells. *The Yale University Library Gazette*. Vol. 64, No. 1/2 (October 1989)

43. Healy, John F. *Pliny the Elder on Science and Technology*. Oxford: Oxford University Press, 1999.

44. Geisler, Norman L., and William E. Nix. *A General Introduction to the Bible*. Chicago: Moody Press, 1968.

45. Ibid.

46. Barnett, Paul. *Is the New Testament Reliable?: A Look at the Historical Evidence*. Downers Grove, Ill.: InterVarsity Press, 1992.

47. Hemer, Colin J., and Conrad H. Gempf. *The Book of Acts in the Setting of Hellenistic History*. Tübingen: J.C.B. Mohr, 1989.

48. Habermas, Gary R. *The Historical Jesus: Ancient Evidence for the Life of Christ*. Joplin, Mo.: College Press Pub., 1996.

49. Quaife, Milo Milton. *Chicago and the Old Northwest, 1673-1835: A Study of the Evolution of the Northwestern Frontier, Together with a History of Fort Dearborn*. Chicago: University of Chicago Press, 1913.

50. John D. Barnhart. *Indiana Magazine of History*. Vol. 41, No. 2 (June, 1945), pp. 187-199

51. Helm, Linai Taliaferro (1912). Gordon, Nelly Kinzie, ed. *The Fort Dearborn Massacre.* Rand, McNally & Company.

52. Mentor L. Williams. *Journal of the Illinois State Historical Society* (1908-1984). Vol. 46, No. 4 (Winter, 1953), pp. 343-362.

53. Habermas, Gary R., and Mike Licona. *The Case for the Resurrection of Jesus.* Grand Rapids, Mich.: Kregel Publications, 2004.

54. Charles Colson, "An Unholy Hoax?" *Breakpoint Commentary*, March 29, 2002 (No. 020339),

55. Geisler, Norman L., and Frank Turek. *I Don't Have Enough Faith to be an Atheist*. Wheaton, Ill.: Crossway Books, 2004.

56. Ibid.

57.   Ibid.

58.   Ibid.

59.   Kinzie, Juliette Augusta Magill (1844). Narrative of the Massacre at Chicago, August 15, 1812, and of some preceding events. Chicago: Ellis & Fergus.

60.   Musham, H. A. (March 1943). "Where Did the Battle of Chicago Take Place?". *Journal of the Illinois State Historical Society*, 36 (1): 21-40.

61.   Loffreda, Stanislao. *Recovering Capharnaum*. Jerusalem: Edizioni Custodia Terra Santa, 1984. ASIN B0007BOTZY.

62.   Hanson, K. C., and Douglas E. Oakman. *Palestine in the Time of Jesus: Social Structures and Social Conflicts*. Minneapolis: Fortress Press, 1998.

63.   "BAR 41:03 | The BAS Library." Biblical Archeological Society. September 30, 1992. Accessed April 23, 2015.

64.   Rosenfeld, Amnon; Feldman, Howard R.; Krumbein, Wolfgang E. (2014). "The Authenticity of the James Ossuary". *Open Journal of Geology*, 4 (3): 69-78.

65.   Lack, David Lambert. *Darwin's Finches: An Essay on the General Biological Theory of Evolution*. New York: Harper, 1961.

66.   Rose, M. R. (1984). "Artificial selection on a fitness component in Drosophila melanogaster," Evolution 38 (3): 516-526.

67.   Lenski, Richard. "62385.5 Generations of E. Coli Evolution and Counting." Richard Lenski Experimental Evolution. Accessed April 23, 2015. http://myxo.css.msu.edu/index.html.

68. Behe, Michael J. *Darwin's Black Box: The Biochemical Challenge to Evolution*. New York: Free, 1996.

69. "Definition of Mathematics in English:." Mathematics: Definition of Mathematics in Oxford Dictionary (American English) (US). Accessed April 23, 2015.

70. Turek, Frank. *Stealing from God: Why Atheists Need God to Make Their Case*. New York: NavPress, 2014.

71. Skeel, David A. *True Paradox: How Christianity Makes Sense of Our Complex World*. New York: IVP Books, 2014.

72. Pascal, Blaise, and W. F. Trotter. *Penses*. Mineola, N.Y.: Dover Publications, 2003.

73. Turek, Frank. *Stealing from God: Why Atheists Need God to Make Their Case*. New York: NavPress, 2014.

74. Albert Speer. (1997). *Inside the Third Reich: Memoirs*. New York: Simon and Schuster.

75. Fred Taylor Translation; *The Goebbels Diaries 1939–41*; Hamish Hamilton Ltd: London; 1982.

76. Sharkey, Word for Word/The Case Against the Nazis; How Hitler's Forces Planned To Destroy German Christianity, New York Times, 13 January 2002.

77. Alan Bullock; *Hitler: A Study in Tyranny*; HarperPerennial Edition 1991.

78. Shirer, William L., *Rise and Fall of the Third Reich: A History of Nazi Germany*, Simon and Schuster, 1990.

79. Fischel, Jack R., *Historical Dictionary of the Holocaust*, Scarecrow Press, 2010.

80. Gill, Anton (1994). *An Honourable Defeat; A History of the German Resistance to Hitler*. Heinemann Mandarin. 1995.

81. Mosse, George Lachmann. *Nazi culture: intellectual, cultural and social life in the Third Reich*, University of Wisconsin Press, 2003.

82. Wheaton, Eliot Barculo. *The Nazi Revolution, 1933–1935: Prelude to calamity: With a background survey of the Weimar era*. New York: Doubleday, 1968.

83. Bendersky, Joseph W., *A concise history of Nazi Germany*, Rowman & Littlefield, 2007.

84. White, Matthew. *Atrocities: The 100 Deadliest Episodes in Human History*. New York: W.W. Norton, 2013.

85. J.B. Hennessey, *Palestine Exploration Quarterly*. (January 1966)

86. Zacharias, Ravi K., and Vince Vitale. *Why Suffering?: Finding Meaning and Comfort When Life Doesn't Make Sense*. Nashville: FaithWords, 2014.

87. "Frank Turek - Mom Plays God: Brings Good from Evil." Townhall.com. April 24, 2011. Accessed April 24, 2015.

88. Wrasman, Andy. *Contradict: They Can't All be True*. Bloomington: West Bow Press, 2014.

89. Turek, Frank. "Apologetics 315." Telephone interview by Brian Auten. March 7, 2013.

www.ingramcontent.com/pod-product-compliance
Lightning Source LLC
Chambersburg PA
CBHW081146040426
42445CB00015B/1789